The Law and Business of Book Copyright (2025 Edition)

Azhar ul Haque Sario

Copyright

First Printing, 2025

Azhar.sario@hotmail.co.uk

ORCID: https://orcid.org/0009-0004-8629-830X
LinkedIn: https://www.linkedin.com/in/azharulhaquesario/

Disclaimer: This book is free from AI use. The cover was designed in Microsoft PowerPoint.

Disclaimer: The author is not affiliated with any national copyright office or board. This book is an independent publication produced under the principle of nominative fair use for commentary and educational purposes.

Contents

Part I: The Foundations of Copyright

The Bedrock of a Book's Value: Understanding Copyright Fundamentals

The Bedrock of a Book's Value: Understanding Copyright Fundamentals

Copyright is not just a legal technicality; it's the engine of the entire literary economy. It's the invisible framework that allows an author to turn a blend of imagination and hard work—something utterly intangible—into an asset that can be bought, sold, licensed, and protected. This legal concept is the fundamental bedrock on which a book's value is built.

At its heart, copyright is a grand bargain. It grants creators a temporary monopoly, a set of "exclusive rights" to their original works. This reward system is designed to incentivize authors, artists, and musicians to create, knowing they can earn a living from their efforts. But this bargain is carefully balanced. This chapter is designed to demystify these core concepts, to show how copyright acts as both a powerful shield for a creator's work and a vital engine for the culture that work hopes to join.

Sub-topic 1.1: The Idea/Expression Dichotomy: Protecting the "How," Not the "What"

This is the single most important principle in all of copyright law.

If you understand this one concept, you understand the entire philosophy behind creative law. It's called the idea-expression dichotomy, and it's a simple, powerful line drawn in the sand.

Here it is: Copyright protects the expression of an idea, but it never protects the idea itself.

It protects the "how," not the "what."

This isn't just a philosophical guideline; it's a hard-and-fast legal rule. The United States Copyright Act, in Section 102(b), carves this out explicitly. It states that copyright protection does not, under any circumstances, "extend to any idea, procedure, process, system, method of operation, concept, principle, or discovery." Other countries follow the exact same logic. Australian law, for example, is clear that copyright protects the "particular form of language" used, not the facts or information themselves.

Think of creativity as a giant, shared sandbox. The ideas in that sandbox—love, war, magic, betrayal, the heroic quest—are the public's sand. Everyone gets to play with them. Everyone can build with them. Copyright law exists to protect the unique, specific castle you build from that sand. It doesn't let you claim ownership of the sand itself.

Why This Line Is So Important

Imagine for a moment if this rule didn't exist.

What if the first author to write about a "young wizard attending a magical school" could copyright that idea? J.K. Rowling's Harry Potter series would have been the first and the last. There would be no The Magicians by Lev Grossman, no A Wizard of Earthsea by Ursula K. Le Guin (which actually came first and explored the concept differently), no Worst Witch by Jill Murphy. The entire "magical school" genre would be the private property of one person.

What if the first author to write a "detective story" could own the concept of a brilliant, troubled sleuth solving a crime? We would have had Sherlock Holmes, and then... nothing. No Sam Spade, no Philip Marlowe, no Hercule Poirot, no modern forensic thrillers.

This is why the idea-expression dichotomy is the engine of culture. It prevents the monopolization of thought. It ensures that the raw materials of creativity—the themes, facts, concepts, and genres—remain in the public commons, available for every new generation of creators to reinterpret, challenge, and build upon. The law rewards your unique labor in crafting a story, not your "eureka moment" of having an idea.

What Is an "Idea"? (What You Can't Protect)

Let's get specific. When the law says "ideas" are free, it means a surprisingly large category of things. This is the "unprotectable" list.

Themes: You cannot copyright the theme of "love conquers all," "the corrupting influence of power," or "man vs. nature."

Concepts & Plots: The idea of a star-crossed romance between feuding families is not protected. That's why we can have both Romeo and Juliet and West Side Story. The idea of a group of friends on a journey to fight a cosmic evil is free, which is why Madeleine L'Engle's A Wrinkle in Time is protected for its expression, not its concept.

Historical Facts: This is a big one. Facts are facts. They belong to everyone. An author can spend a decade researching the Civil War. They can unearth new letters and documents. But they cannot copyright the facts they discover. Anyone else is free to use those same facts (the dates, the names, the troop movements) in their own book.

Scientific Discoveries: You can't copyright gravity. You can't copyright the discovery that a certain mold kills bacteria. You can get a patent for a new machine or chemical process, but the discovery itself—the raw knowledge—is a fact that becomes public property.

Systems & Processes: This is where the Baker v. Selden case from 1879 set the standard. A man named Selden created a new, more efficient system of accounting and published a book explaining it, complete with blank forms. Baker created his own book using a very similar system. Selden sued. The Supreme Court ruled that the system of accounting was an unprotectable idea or method. To give Selden a copyright on his forms—the essential tool for using the system—would be the same as giving him a monopoly on the system itself. This is why you can't copyright a list of ingredients in a recipe. The list is a process. You can, however, copyright the expression—the descriptive text, the helpful hints, the personal story about your grandmother that you include with the recipe.

What Is an "Expression"? (What You Can Protect)

This is what you, the creator, get to own. This is your property.

Your Specific Words: The literal prose. The way you arrange sentences, your unique metaphors, your descriptive language, your specific dialogue. This is the most basic level of expression.

The "Selection and Arrangement": This is a more subtle, but powerful, form of expression. It's especially important for non-fiction. Let's go back to that Civil War historian. They can't copyright the facts. But what can they copyright? Their expression of those facts. This includes:

Selection: From the mountain of available facts, which ones did they choose to include? Which did they omit?

Arrangement: How did they organize the facts? Did they tell the story chronologically? Did they structure the book around specific themes (e.g., "The Soldier's Experience," "The Political Battle")?

Narrative: How did they weave these facts into a compelling story? What was their "take" or argument?

Two historians can start with the exact same set of historical records and write two completely different, and independently copyrighted, books. They are free to copy the facts from each other, but not the expression. This is why Ernest Hemingway's A Farewell to Arms (which entered the U.S. public domain in 2025) was protected.

Anyone could write a novel about the Italian front in World War I—that's an idea and a set of facts. But only Hemingway could write that specific story, with those characters and that iconic, sparse prose.

"Highly Delineated" Characters: A "stock character" is an unprotectable idea. A "grumpy old mentor," a "rebellious teen," or a "hard-boiled detective" are all free to use. But when does a character cross the line from a stock "idea" to a protected "expression"? The answer is when they are "fully delineated"—when they have so much specific, unique detail (their appearance, their backstory, their voice, their consistent ticks and habits) that they feel like a real person. A "boy wizard" is an idea. Harry Potter—with his lightning-bolt scar, his broken glasses, his specific parentage, and his membership in Gryffindor—is a protected expression.

Intricate Plot Details: A "quest" is an idea. But the specific, detailed, and often arbitrary sequence of events in a novel is a protected expression. The idea of a journey to destroy a magic ring is not protected. The plot of The Lord of the Rings—involving Hobbits, the specific formation of the Fellowship, the journey through Moria, the encounter with Shelob, the specific role of Gollum—is a highly protected, complex expression.

The Blurry Lines: Where Idea and Expression Get Complicated

This all sounds clear-cut, but in the real world, the line can get very blurry. Courts have developed two other concepts to help patrol this border.

The Scènes à Faire Doctrine: This is a French term that means "scenes that must be done" or "scenes that are indispensable." This doctrine says that certain elements, themes, and plot devices are so common and expected within a specific genre that they are considered unprotectable ideas, even if they look like expression.

In a 1980s action movie, you expect a car chase, a training montage, and a final showdown with the main villain.

In a gritty detective novel, you expect a smoky office, a femme fatale client, a corrupt cop, and a few fistfights in a dark alley.

In a vampire story, you expect fangs, blood-drinking, a fear of sunlight, and coffins.

You cannot sue another author for using these elements. They are the "stock" ingredients of the genre. They are part of the shared "idea" of a vampire story or a detective novel, and they are free for all to use.

The Merger Doctrine: This is the most advanced concept, and it's fascinating. The merger doctrine says that sometimes, an idea can only be expressed in one or two ways. When this happens, the law says the idea and the expression have "merged." And since the law never protects an idea, it will refuse to protect the expression either.

Why? Because to protect that one, simple expression would be the same as giving the author a monopoly on the idea itself.

The classic example is a rule for a contest. The idea is "entrants must be 21 years or older." How many ways can you say that?

"Must be 21 to enter."

"Entry limited to persons 21 and over."

"You must be 21 years old to participate."

There are only a few simple, functional ways to state this rule. A court would rule that the idea (the rule) and the expression (the short sentence) have merged. Therefore, no protection. You can't sue someone for using the phrase "Must be 21 to enter."

This doctrine also applies to simple facts. If you are writing about a blank, functional form, like the one in Baker v. Selden, the "expression" of the form is the "idea" of the system. They have merged, and there is no copyright.

The Final Balance: An Engine for Progress

This is the great, delicate balancing act of copyright. The idea-expression dichotomy is the central gear in this machine.

It is designed to give authors a powerful shield. This shield protects your unique words, your narrative structure, and your complex characters. It gives you the economic power to profit from your specific, tangible work.

At the exact same time, it is designed to leave the world of ideas completely, radically, and beautifully free. It leaves the facts of history, the truths of science, the themes of human existence, and the concepts of genre in the public sandbox.

This dual role is copyright's greatest gift. It ensures that every new book, every new film, and every new song has a solid financial and legal foundation, while simultaneously guaranteeing that the next creator will always have the raw materials they need to build something new.

The First Pillar: The Threshold of Originality

Copyright law is built on two fundamental pillars. Without them, the entire structure of creative protection simply doesn't exist. The first of these pillars is originality. This single word is perhaps the most important, and often the most misunderstood, concept in all of copyright. When we hear "original," we often think of something brand new, groundbreaking, or artistically brilliant. We think of a completely novel idea. But in the world of copyright, "originality" means something much simpler and far more accessible.

The threshold for originality is, by design, incredibly low. The law does not want to be an art critic. It doesn't want to be in the business of deciding what is "good" art or "bad" art. A child's crayon drawing is, in the eyes of copyright law, just as protectable as a masterpiece hanging in the Louvre, assuming it meets the originality test. The law also doesn't care if the work is "novel" or "ingenious"—those are requirements for patent law, which protects inventions. Copyright protects expression.

So, what does originality mean? It boils down to two simple things:

Independent Creation: The work must have been independently created by its author. It must originate from you.

Minimal Creativity: The work must possess at least a "minimal degree of creativity."

Let's break that down. "Independent creation" simply means you didn't copy it from someone else. If you and your neighbor, living on opposite sides of the country and with no contact, somehow write the exact same 12-line poem, both poems are considered "original." Neither of you copied the other. The work originated from each of you independently. This is a far cry from "novelty," which would imply the poem had never existed before in human history. Copyright doesn't care about that. It only cares that you didn't cheat. This is why it's often said the work must not be a "slavish copy" of another. If all you do is trace another person's drawing or re-type their novel word-for-word, you have not created anything; you have merely reproduced it. Your work lacks an independent origin.

The second part, "minimal creativity," is where things get slightly more defined. The U.S. Supreme Court, in a landmark case (Feist Publications, Inc. v. Rural Telephone Service Co.), famously described this as needing a "spark" or a "modicum" of creativity. This is a deliberately tiny hurdle. It means that the work can't be purely mechanical, automatic, or dictated by rules.

The Feist case is the perfect example. It involved phone books. One company (Rural) published a standard white-pages phone book. Another company (Feist) wanted to use that data for its own regional directory. Feist copied Rural's listings, and Rural sued for copyright infringement. The Supreme Court sided with Feist. Why? It ruled that Rural's white pages—a simple, alphabetical listing of all phone subscribers—was not original. There was no "spark" of creativity in arranging names alphabetically. That's a standard, mechanical process. It's an idea, a method. The court said that the "sweat of the brow," or the sheer effort of collecting the data, doesn't equal creativity.

This brings us to a critical distinction: Copyright does not protect facts or ideas. It only protects the expression of those facts or ideas. You cannot copyright the fact that the sky is blue. You cannot copyright the idea of a mystery novel set on a train. But you can copyright your specific paragraph describing the blue sky, with its unique word choice and "spark" of creativity. You can copyright your novel, Murder on the Orient Express, which is a specific expression of that idea.

Where does that "spark" come from? It comes from choices. When an author selects which facts to include in a history book, how to arrange them to tell a story, and what language to use to describe them, that is originality. When a photographer decides on the lighting, the angle, the composition, and the exact moment to click the shutter, that is originality. Even a simple snapshot can have it.

The bar is so low that almost anything that a human produces will pass it. A grocery list probably doesn't (it's a mere list of facts, like a phone book). But a description of a grocery list, or a list arranged in a poetic or funny way, almost certainly would.

Finally, there's the implicit element mentioned in the text: the work must be created by a human author. This has become a red-hot topic in the age of artificial intelligence. Based on legal precedent, such as the famous "monkey selfie" case (where a court ruled a monkey couldn't own a copyright), and recent guidance from copyright offices, the "spark" of creativity must originate from a human mind. A work generated 100% by an AI, without human creative input or direction, would fail the originality test because it lacks a human author. Originality, at its core, is a celebration of the unique, creative choices—however small—that only a human mind can make.

The Second Pillar: The Mandate of Fixation

If originality is the "soul" of the work, the second pillar, fixation, is its "body." This requirement is just as important, and it draws a bright, clear line between a mere idea and a protectable piece of property. The law is very clear: Copyright does not protect ideas. It protects the expression of ideas, and only when that expression is "fixed in a tangible medium."

What does this mean? It means the work must be captured, stored, or recorded in a form that is solid enough for it to be perceived, reproduced, or communicated for more than a brief, fleeting moment. It's the act of taking something from your mind and making it "real" in the physical or digital world.

Let's use the prompt's excellent example of the poet. The poet stands on stage and recites a brilliant new poem they just thought of. Is the poem protected by copyright? No. Not yet. At that moment, the poem exists only as sound waves traveling through the air and as a memory in the minds of the audience. It is not "fixed." It's what the law calls "transitory." It's fleeting. As soon as the poet stops speaking, the sound waves are gone. You can't press "rewind" on the air itself.

But the instant that poet does one of several things, the legal landscape changes completely:

The poet writes the poem on a napkin.

The poet types it into a note-taking app on their phone and hits "save."

A member of the audience hits the "record" button on their phone's audio recorder.

The poet goes home and types it into a word processor and saves the file.

In all of these cases, the poem has now been fixed. The napkin, the phone's flash memory, and the computer's hard drive are all "tangible media of expression." The work is no longer just an idea or a performance; it is a stable, recorded thing. From this thing, the poem can be perceived (read), reproduced (photocopied, re-typed), or communicated (read aloud again).

This requirement of fixation is what separates the idea of a story from the novel itself. You can have a detailed, brilliant idea for a 10-book fantasy series in your head. You can tell your friends all about it over dinner. You have zero copyright protection. None. If one of your friends goes home and writes that novel themselves, they haven't infringed your copyright, because you didn't have one. They have only taken your idea—which is perfectly legal. But the moment you write Chapter 1 and save the file, that file—that specific expression of your idea—is protected.

The definition of "tangible medium" is incredibly broad, especially today. It covers:

Traditional Media: Paper, canvas, photographic film, musical scores, marble (for a sculpture).

Digital Media: Hard drives, solid-state drives (SSDs), USB flash drives, memory cards, a server on the internet, a file saved in the cloud.

Recording Media: Audio tape, vinyl records, CDs, DVDs, digital audio files (MP3s), digital video files (MP4s).

The key is that the work must be stable enough for "more than a transitory period." A live, unrecorded television broadcast is a classic example of something not fixed. The images are just electronic signals that vanish. But the moment that broadcast is recorded—by the TV station or even by you on your home DVR—it becomes a fixed work.

This leads to one of the most important practical realities of copyright law. The very moment a work is both original (has that human spark) and fixed (is saved or recorded), it is automatically protected by copyright.

You do not need to do anything else. You don't have to file a form. You don't have to mail a copy to yourself (that's a popular myth). You don't have to publish it. You don't even have to put the little © symbol on it.

This automatic protection is a central part of international copyright law (thanks to the Berne Convention, which most countries have signed). The instant you finish your song and save the audio file, the instant you take a photo and it saves to your camera's memory card, the instant you finish your painting—BAM. You are the copyright owner.

Now, there is a separate concept of registering your copyright, for example, with the U.S. Copyright Office. Registration is not required for protection to exist, but it's a very good idea. Registration is a legal formality that gives you major advantages if you ever have to go to court to sue someone for stealing your work. For instance, in the U.S., you generally must have a registration (or have applied for one) before you can file an infringement lawsuit. It also makes you eligible for certain types of high-value damages.

But the protection itself? The fundamental right to call that work yours? That happens automatically. It's the magic moment where the two pillars click into place: your human originality meets tangible fixation.

The Great Copyright Misconception

It's one of the most common points of confusion for any creator. You've just finished your masterpiece—a novel, a song, a screenplay. You've poured your soul into it. And you've come up with the perfect title. It's brilliant, it's catchy, it's original. So, naturally, you want to copyright it. You want to own it, to protect it from anyone else who might dare to use it.

This is a completely logical instinct. Unfortunately, in the eyes of the law, it's almost entirely incorrect.

This is where many creative journeys hit their first legal roadblock. The hard truth is that copyright does not protect titles, names, short phrases, or slogans. This is a fundamental rule, and understanding it is just as important as knowing what copyright does protect (like your actual book, song, or film).

This isn't some arbitrary loophole. There are very specific, foundational reasons why the legal system draws this line. It all comes down to the core purpose of copyright itself and a simple, vital concept: originality.

Why Copyright Says No: The "Spark" of Creativity

To understand what copyright doesn't protect, we have to first remember what it does protect. Copyright law is designed to protect "original works of authorship fixed in a tangible medium of expression."

Let's break that down. "Fixed in a tangible medium" is easy. It just means written down, recorded, saved on a hard drive, or painted on a canvas. It's not just an idea in your head.

The key word, the one that causes all the trouble, is "original."

The legal system has a specific bar for what it considers "original." It doesn't mean "good" or "novel" or "clever." It means the work possesses at least a de minimis—a minimal, tiny spark—of human-authored creativity. It's a very low bar, but it is a bar.

Your 400-page novel easily clears this bar. Your three-verse song clears it. Your 90-minute screenplay clears it.

A title, however, almost never does.

The U.S. Copyright Office is incredibly clear on this. In its official circulars, it states that "words and short phrases, such as names, titles, and slogans" are not copyrightable. They are seen as lacking the "minimum amount of authorship" required to qualify for protection.

Think of it this way: copyright protects the vast, complex creative expression inside the book. It does not protect the simple, functional label you put on the cover to tell people what it is. A title is seen as a tool for identification, not a creative work in itself.

The Case of Titles: Labels, Not Literature

This is where creators often get frustrated. What about a title like William Faulkner's The Sound and the Fury? That's creative, isn't it? It's a poetic quote from Shakespeare.

Yes, it is. But it's still just a short phrase. It's not the work itself. As the provided text correctly notes, any author in the world could, in theory, publish a brand-new, completely unrelated novel tomorrow and also call it The Sound and the Fury. They would not be infringing on Faulkner's copyright because the title itself was never protected by it.

We see this all the time. Go to a bookstore or search online. You will find multiple, unrelated books with titles like "The Gift," "Twilight," "Sanctuary," or "Crossroads." This is perfectly legal.

The Merger Doctrine: When an Idea and a Title Are One

There's another important legal concept at play here called the "merger doctrine." This doctrine says that if an idea and its expression are so tied together that there are only one or a very few ways to say it, the expression "merges" with the idea. And since ideas cannot be copyrighted, the expression can't be, either.

Titles are a classic example.

Imagine you write a book called "How to Bake Bread." Could you copyright that title? If you could, you would effectively own a monopoly on the very idea of a book that teaches bread-baking. No one else could label their bread-baking book in a clear, descriptive way. The law says no. The title "How to Bake Bread" has merged with the idea it describes, so it's free for everyone to use.

The same goes for "The Murder Mystery," "A Love Story," or "My Biography." These titles are simple descriptions. They are functional. They are labels. They are not the "original work of authorship" that copyright is designed to protect. Granting a copyright on them would stifle, not promote, creativity.

The Nuance of Names: Protecting the Character, Not the Word

"Okay," you might say, "I get titles. But what about my character's name? I invented 'Xylo Zephyr' for my sci-fi epic. That's original!"

This is the most nuanced part of the rule, and it requires making a very careful distinction. Just like a title, the name "Xylo Zephyr" by itself is not copyrightable. Neither is "James Bond," "Superman," or "Harry Potter." They are just names. They are short phrases.

So, what is protected?

The character, as a fully-expressed creation, is protected by copyright.

This is the vital difference. You don't have a copyright on the name "James Bond." You have a copyright on the specific, "sufficiently delineated" character who is a sophisticated, cold-blooded British secret agent, license to kill, who loves martinis (shaken, not stirred), drives an Aston Martin, and has a particular set of mannerisms and backstory.

Courts use a test for this. Is the character just a "stock" character (e.g., "a grizzled detective," "a plucky sidekick")? If so, not much protection. But is the character "especially distinctive" and "fully developed" to the point where they "constitute the story being told"? If yes, that character is a "work of authorship" and is protected by copyright.

This protection is so strong it can even extend to non-human "characters." In legal cases, courts have held that the Batmobile is a copyrightable character. The Klingon species from Star Trek, with their detailed language, culture, and ridged foreheads, have been found to be protectable.

So, while you can't stop someone from creating a new, unrelated character also named Xylo Zephyr, you can stop them from copying your Xylo Zephyr—his personality, his backstory, his unique powers, and his specific way of speaking. You own the expression, not the name.

Short Phrases and Slogans: Too Small to Protect

This same logic applies directly to short phrases and slogans. This is why you cannot copyright "Just Do It," "I'm Lovin' It," or "Where's the Beef?"

These phrases may be incredibly clever, famous, and valuable, but in the eyes of copyright law, they are de minimis. They're simply too short and lack the minimal creative spark. They're seen as "trivial variations" of common words that belong to the public.

A famous legal scholar, Melville Nimmer, put it best: "The smaller the effort... the greater must be the degree of creativity in order to claim copyright protection." The bar for a tiny phrase is, therefore, impossibly high.

These phrases are not orphans, however. They are just protected by a different law.

The Real Protector: Trademark Law

This is where the confusion from the original prompt finally gets resolved. If copyright won't protect your title, name, or slogan, what will?

The answer is trademark.

It is absolutely crucial to understand the difference.

Copyright protects creative works of authorship (the book, the song, the painting).

Trademark protects brand identifiers (words, symbols, or phrases that identify the source of goods or services).

A trademark's entire job is to prevent consumer confusion. When you see the word "Nike" on a shoe, trademark law ensures that you are getting a real shoe from the Nike company, not a fake from someone else. When you see "Coca-Cola" on a can, you know what you're getting.

This is exactly how series titles and major character names are protected.

The name "Harry Potter" is one of the most valuable trademarks on Earth. It is not protected by copyright. It is protected by trademark because, in the minds of consumers, those two words have one single meaning: they identify a specific series of books, films, and merchandise all coming from a single source (J.K. Rowling and her partner companies).

If another publisher tried to release a new fantasy series called "The Adventures of Harry Potter," they would be sued for trademark infringement, not copyright infringement. The argument would be that they are intentionally confusing consumers into thinking their product is an official part of the "Harry Potter" brand.

This is why series titles are often trademarked ("Chicken Soup for the Soul," "For Dummies"), while single book titles are usually not. A series title functions as a brand. A single book title is usually just seen as the descriptive name of one product.

The "Secondary Meaning" Hurdle

So, can a single book title ever be protected? Yes, but it's very difficult. It has to clear a high legal hurdle called "secondary meaning."

"Secondary meaning" is a legal term that means a title has become so famous, through sales, marketing, and time, that the public no longer thinks of the words' primary, literal meaning. Instead, they immediately associate that title with one specific book or film.

"Gone with the Wind" no longer just means a breeze is gone. It means that specific story.

"Jaws" no longer just means the mouth of an animal. It means that specific shark movie.

These titles have acquired "secondary meaning" and function as trademarks for that single work.

This is a high bar. Your new novel, "The Girl on the Train," does not have secondary meaning. (In fact, there were several books with that title). But Paula Hawkins's massive bestseller? It has arguably achieved secondary meaning through its global brand recognition.

Even without a registered trademark, a title that has acquired secondary meaning can often be defended in court under the common-law doctrine of "unfair competition." This is a legal claim that stops a competitor from "passing off" their work as yours by using a confusingly similar title to ride on your success.

A Creator's Toolkit: Using the Right Law

Understanding this distinction is not just academic. It's a vital part of a creator's professional toolkit.

Worrying about someone "stealing" your title is a waste of creative energy. The law is clear: you can't protect it with copyright. Instead, you should focus your energy on what you can protect.

Protect your work with Copyright. Your protection for your book, song, or script is automatic the moment you "fix" it in a tangible form. Registering it with the U.S. Copyright Office just gives you stronger legal tools if you ever need to sue. This copyright protects the content—the 100,000 words you wrote, the melody you composed, the scenes you structured.

Protect your brand with Trademark. If you are building a series, a brand, or a character that you plan to license, that's when you think about trademark. Are you writing "The Xylo Zephyr Chronicles"? That series title is what you would file a trademark application for. This protects the brand name and stops others from creating a "Xylo Zephyr" product that confuses your audience.

In the end, copyright and trademark are two different tools for two different jobs. Copyright protects the art you create. Trademark protects the brand you build. Titles, names, and slogans fall squarely into the world of branding, and it's essential for creators to know the difference.

The Copyright Bargain: Fostering Progress by Balancing Creator Incentives and Public Access

Copyright is one of the most pervasive and misunderstood legal concepts in our modern world. We interact with it every single day, from the music we stream, to the books we read, the software on our computers, and the movies we watch. At its core, copyright is not a simple, absolute right of ownership. It is a complex, carefully constructed bargain between the public and the creator. This bargain has a single, vital purpose: "To promote the Progress of Science and useful Arts."

This foundational goal, enshrined in the U.S. Constitution, reveals the entire story. Society agrees to grant creators a temporary, limited monopoly over their original works. This monopoly is the "incentive" part of the equation. It allows an author, musician, or filmmaker to profit from their labor. But this monopoly is not forever, and it is not absolute. It is balanced against the public's profound interest in accessing, sharing, and building upon those works. This is the "public access" side of the bargain.

Understanding copyright means understanding this delicate balance. It is not a law designed purely to make creators rich, nor is it a law designed to make all information free. It is a pragmatic policy tool, a piece of economic and cultural engineering designed to foster a vibrant, creative ecosystem where new works are continuously produced and our shared well of knowledge is continuously enriched. This essay will explore the two sides of this fundamental bargain: first, the economic and moral justifications for providing incentives to creators, and second, the equally important legal doctrines that limit those incentives to protect the public good.

Part 1: The Engine of Creation: Securing the Creator's Incentive

The first half of the copyright bargain is the incentive. Why does society need to grant a right for someone to control their own work? The answer lies in the unique nature of creative works and the economics of information.

The Economics of a Public Good

A creative work, like a song or a story, is what economists call a "public good." This means it has two specific properties. First, it is "non-rivalrous," meaning one person's consumption of it doesn't prevent another person from also consuming it. We can both listen to the same song without using it up. Second, without a legal framework, it is "non-excludable." Once a work is made public, it is incredibly easy to copy and share, making it difficult to "exclude" people who haven't paid for it.

This creates a classic market failure. Imagine a novelist who spends two years writing a book. On the day it's published, a third party buys one copy, photocopies it, and starts selling it for a tenth of the price. The original author, who bore all the costs of creation (time, research, living expenses), cannot compete with a copier who had zero costs. In a world without copyright, this would be the norm.

Faced with this reality, very few people could afford to dedicate their lives to creating complex, time-consuming works. The "starving artist" would be the default, and major creative industries—publishing, film, music, software—

simply would not exist at their current scale. The incentive to create, at least professionally, would evaporate.

Copyright as a Solution: The "Limited Monopoly"

Copyright law solves this problem by making the "non-excludable" work excludable again, at least for a while. It grants the author a "bundle of rights" for a "limited time." These exclusive rights are the core of the incentive. They typically include the right to:

Reproduce the work (e.g., print copies of a book, press copies of a CD).

Distribute the work (e.g., sell the book in a store, stream the song).

Create derivative works (e.g., make a movie based on the novel, create a remix of a song).

Perform the work publicly (e.g., stage a play, broadcast a song on the radio).

Display the work publicly (e.g., show a painting in a gallery, project a photograph).

These rights transform the creative work from an intangible public good into a marketable asset. The author can now sell or license these rights. A novelist can license the reproduction right to a publisher, the derivative right to a movie studio, and the public performance right to an audiobook producer. Each of these licenses provides a stream of revenue, creating a "fair return for an author's creative labor."

Beyond the Author: Incentivizing Investment

This economic incentive is not just for the individual creator. It is essential for the entire creative ecosystem. A major motion picture can cost hundreds of millions of dollars. A complex software program or a new video game can require a team of hundreds and years of development.

No publisher, studio, or tech company would make these massive, high-risk investments if their finished product could be legally copied and distributed for free by competitors the moment it was released. Copyright protection provides the "security" mentioned in the Constitution. It secures the potential for a return on investment, which in turn unlocks the capital needed to fund large-scale creative and scientific projects.

This system is deliberately designed to stimulate artistic creativity. It provides the economic foundation for a professional class of creators and the industries that support them. The ultimate beneficiary, in theory, is the public, which gets to enjoy a vast and diverse array of new books, films, music, and art that might otherwise never have been made. This is the "ultimate benefit of the public good."

The Moral Argument for Copyright

While the U.S. constitutional framing is openly utilitarian—it's a tool for "Progress"—there is also a philosophical or "moral" argument for copyright. This view, more common in European legal traditions, is rooted in the idea of natural rights. It holds that an author has a natural, moral right to the "fruits of their labor."

Just as a carpenter has a right to the chair they build, a writer has a right to the story they create. It is seen as an extension of their personality and intellect. This perspective frames copyright less as a government-granted incentive and more as a fundamental property right. While the U.S. system ultimately prioritizes the public benefit, this moral dimension adds weight to the importance of protecting an author's work and securing a fair return for their efforts.

Part 2: The Public's Share: Access, Knowledge, and the Commons

The incentive to create is powerful, but it is only half of the bargain. The Constitution makes it clear that the goal is "Progress," not just payment. An incentive system that locked away all new works forever would stifle progress, not promote it.

If copyright were absolute, it would impede the "harvest of knowledge." Every creator is also a consumer of culture. We all stand on the shoulders of giants. The creators of West Side Story needed access to Romeo and Juliet. Scientists must be able to cite, critique, and build upon the research of their peers. Progress depends on a rich and accessible public sphere of knowledge and culture.

To protect this public interest, copyright law has several crucial, built-in limitations. These limitations are not loopholes; they are essential features of the system, just as important as the exclusive rights themselves.

1. The Idea-Expression Dichotomy

This is perhaps the most important limitation in all of copyright. Copyright law protects the expression of an idea, but never the idea itself. It protects the specific words used to tell a story, but not the plot. It protects a specific melody, but not the underlying chord progression. It protects a block of software code, but not the algorithm or function it performs.

This distinction is fundamental to a free and competitive creative landscape. For example, the idea of a boy wizard attending a magic school to fight a dark lord is not protected by copyright. This allows other authors to write their own, different stories about boy wizards, like The Magicians or A Wizard of Earthsea. What is protected is the specific expression—the characters, text, and specific plot points of Harry Potter.

Similarly, the idea of a "zombie apocalypse" is free for anyone to use. This allows for a multitude of books, movies, and shows based on this single concept, from The Walking Dead to The Last of Us, each with its own unique expression. If the first person to write a zombie story could copyright the idea of zombies, it would have created a creative dead end. The idea-expression dichotomy ensures that foundational concepts, facts, and genres remain free for all to use as building blocks for new works.

2. The "Limited Times" and the Public Domain

The Constitution explicitly states that the monopoly is for "limited Times." This is a non-negotiable part of the bargain. Every copyrighted work, without exception, will one day see its copyright expire. When it does, the work enters the public domain.

The public domain is our shared cultural heritage. It is a vast, ever-growing commons of creativity that belongs to everyone. It includes all the works of Shakespeare, the music of Mozart and Beethoven, the paintings of da Vinci, and, as of recently, early iconic works like the first Mickey Mouse cartoon, Steamboat Willie.

Once a work is in the public domain, it is free. Anyone can use it, adapt it, republish it, or build upon it for any purpose without permission and without payment. This is why you can buy dozens of different editions of Pride and Prejudice. It's why Disney was able to freely adapt public domain fairy tales like Cinderella and Snow White. The public domain is the engine that fuels future generations of creators. It is the ultimate "return" on the public's investment, ensuring that the temporary monopoly eventually enriches our shared culture permanently.

3. Fair Use and Fair Dealing

Finally, what about works that are still under copyright? Does the public have any rights to use them? Yes. The most important of these rights in the U.S. is the doctrine of fair use. (Other countries have similar, though often more restrictive, concepts like "fair dealing.")

Fair use is a flexible "safety valve" that ensures the public can make certain uses of copyrighted works without permission for purposes that serve the public interest. These purposes include criticism, commentary, news reporting, teaching, scholarship, and research. It recognizes that a rigid monopoly would stifle the very "Progress" it's meant to promote.

Fair use is what allows a book critic to quote passages from a new novel in a review. It allows a movie reviewer to show short clips in their video essay. It allows a teacher to photocopy a poem to discuss in class. It is what allows for parody, like the work of "Weird Al" Yankovic, which must use the original work to comment on it.

This doctrine is intentionally flexible, not a set of bright-line rules. It is a balancing test that ensures the monopoly of the copyright holder does not trample on other vital public interests, like free speech, education, and the ability to build upon the culture around us.

Conclusion: A Delicate, Evolving Balance

Copyright law is not, and has never been, an absolute property right. It is a carefully calibrated policy tool. It is a grand bargain, struck to achieve a specific public purpose: the "Progress of Science and useful Arts."

It does this by granting a powerful, temporary monopoly as an economic incentive for creators and investors, ensuring they receive a fair return for their labor and risk. This incentive structure is the engine that funds and professionalizes our creative industries, resulting in a wealth of new works.

But this incentive is carefully and deliberately limited. It is balanced against the public's right to access and build upon our shared culture. This balance is maintained through critical doctrines: the idea-expression dichotomy keeps basic ideas free, the limited duration of copyright guarantees an ever-expanding public domain, and fair use ensures that culture can be discussed, critiqued, and taught even while it is still protected.

This balance is not static. New technologies, from the printing press to the internet and now generative artificial intelligence, constantly test and strain this bargain, forcing society to re-examine where the lines should be drawn. But the fundamental goal remains the same: to foster a vibrant creative ecosystem that enriches both the creators of today and the public of tomorrow, ultimately increasing, not impeding, our collective "harvest of knowledge."

The Global Copyright Compact: The Berne Convention and International Treaties

Sub-topic 2.1: The Berne Convention: Core Principles of National Treatment and Automatic Protection

The Berne Convention is, without exaggeration, the beating heart of the global copyright system. Concluded way back in 1886, it was a revolutionary document, a peace treaty for ideas. Before it existed, a creator's world was small and fraught with peril. An American author's novel could be stolen, reprinted, and sold in Germany with total impunity. A French composer's music could be performed in Italy without permission or payment. The world of creativity was like the Wild West, with border posts acting as the end of all rights. The Berne Convention changed everything. It built a bridge of protection across borders, and it did so using three foundational ideas that remain as powerful today as they were in the 19th century.

The First Pillar: National Treatment

The most important principle, the true cornerstone of the entire structure, is National Treatment.

What does this mean in simple terms? It's a rule of absolute fairness. It commands every member country to give the same level of copyright protection to foreign creators that it gives to its own creators. It is a powerful anti-discrimination clause for the mind. Your passport, your nationality, your country of origin—none of it matters. If your country is a member of the Berne Convention, every other member country must treat you like one of their own.

Let's unpack this. Imagine you are a novelist from Canada. You write a successful book that starts getting sold in France. Suddenly, you discover a French company has copied your book and is selling a cheap, unauthorized version. What can you do? Before Berne, the answer might have been "nothing." But because both Canada and France are members of the Convention, the principle of National Treatment kicks in. You, the Canadian author, have the right to walk into a French court and demand the full protection of French copyright law, just as if you were a famous Parisian author. Whatever rights a French author has against infringement in their own country, you now have those exact same rights.

This leads to a fascinating and critical legal concept mentioned in the text: lex loci delicti. This is a Latin phrase that sounds complex, but its meaning is simple and logical. It means the "law of the place where the wrong was committed." The law that applies is the law of the country where the infringement happened, not the law of the country where the author is from.

Think of it this way: if your book is pirated in France, you use French law. If the same book is pirated in Japan, you use Japanese law. This makes perfect sense. You are seeking protection within a specific country's borders, so you use that country's legal rulebook. This system ensures that every creator, regardless of origin, is on a level playing field within any given member nation.

The Second Pillar: Automatic Protection

The second principle is Automatic Protection, and it is perhaps the most empowering for individual creators.

This principle is radical in its simplicity: copyright protection must not depend on any formal requirements. You don't have to register your work. You don't have to file a form with a government office. You don't have to pay a fee. You don't even have to use the little © copyright symbol.

Protection is automatic.

The moment you create an original work and "fix" it in a tangible medium, it is protected by copyright. Instantly. Globally.

What does "fixed in a tangible medium" mean? It just means the work is no longer only an idea in your head.

The moment you write your poem down on a napkin, it's fixed.

The moment you save your digital photograph to a memory card, it's fixed.

The moment you record your song into your phone's voice memos, it's fixed.

The moment you type "The End" on your screenplay and save the document, it's fixed.

In that very second, your work is fully protected by copyright in your own country and in all 180+ other Berne Convention member nations.

This was a massive shift. Before this, many countries—the United States being a prime example for a very long time—required strict formalities. You had to publish the work with a specific notice (e.g., "Copyright 1950 by Jane Doe"). You had to register it with the Copyright Office. If you made a tiny mistake in the notice or missed a deadline for registration, your work could be thrust into the public domain, free for anyone to use forever. It was a minefield of technicalities that trapped countless unsuspecting authors.

The Berne Convention did away with all of Fthat. It declared that creativity itself was the only requirement. This principle democratized copyright, taking it out of the hands of lawyers and bureaucrats and placing it directly into the hands of authors, artists, musicians, and coders.

The Third Pillar: Independence of Protection

The third principle, Independence of Protection, acts as a crucial firewall.

It states that your copyright protection in one Berne country is completely independent of your protection in any other country, including your own country of origin. Each member nation provides a separate, distinct "bubble" of protection.

Let's use the example from the text. Imagine an author from Country A writes a book. For some strange reason, due to an obscure law in Country A, that book falls into the public domain in Country A. Maybe the author was a government employee, or the work was of a type not protected by that nation's specific laws.

Does this mean the book is now in the public domain everywhere else? Absolutely not.

Thanks to the independence of protection, that same book is still fully protected in Country B, Country C, and Country D for the full term of their copyright laws. The fact that the protection "bubble" popped in Country A has no legal effect on the "bubble" in Country B. This prevents a domino effect where a legal issue in one country could destroy an author's rights across the entire globe.

Together, these three principles—National Treatment, Automatic Protection, and Independence of Protection—create a seamless, powerful, and user-friendly safety net. They ensure that creators are treated fairly, protected instantly, and secured robustly, no matter where their work travels in this interconnected world.

Sub-topic 2.2: Minimum Standards of Protection under Berne

The three core principles of the Berne Convention set up the how of international copyright. They explain how protection works: you get treated like a local (National Treatment), it happens instantly (Automatic Protection), and it's secure in each country (Independence of Protection).

But that's only half the story. The Convention also dictates the what. It establishes a set of minimum standards of protection that every single member country must agree to provide. This is often called a "harmonized floor." A country is free to build above this floor—to offer more protection—but it is not allowed to dig below it. This ensures that an author's rights have a strong, consistent baseline of value and scope, no matter where they are in the world.

These minimum standards cover four critical areas.

1. A Broad Scope for Protectable Works

First, the Berne Convention defines what can be protected in the broadest possible terms. It doesn't list a few specific things like "books and paintings." Instead, it uses sweeping, future-proof language. It mandates that protection must extend to "every production in the literary, scientific and artistic domain, whatever the mode or form of its expression."

This phrasing is brilliant. The authors in 1886 could not possibly have conceived of websites, computer software, video games, streaming films, or digital art. By focusing on "every production" and "whatever the mode or form," they ensured the treaty would not become obsolete with the invention of the next technology.

This means that a novel is protected whether it's a leather-bound book, an e-book file, or an audiobook. A song is protected whether it's written as sheet music, pressed onto a vinyl record, or streamed as an MP3. This expansive definition ensures that as human creativity evolves, the Convention evolves right alongside it, automatically covering new forms of expression.

2. The "Bundle" of Minimum Economic Rights

Second, the Convention lists the minimum set of exclusive economic rights that authors must be granted. These are the rights that allow a creator to control their work and earn a living from it. Think of copyright not as a single thing, but as a "bundle of rights," like a bundle of sticks. The author, as the owner, can keep all the sticks, or they can give some away, or sell them, or license them temporarily.

Berne mandates that this bundle must include at least the following:

The Right of Reproduction: This is the most fundamental right. It's the right to make copies of the work. Printing a book, manufacturing a DVD, or even saving a digital file to a hard drive are all acts of reproduction.

The Right of Translation: An author's work cannot simply be translated into another language and sold without their permission. The original author controls the right to create (or license) a French, Spanish, or Japanese version of their book.

The Right to Make Adaptations: This is the right to create new works based on the original. This is incredibly valuable. Turning a novel into a movie is an adaptation. Turning a play into a musical is an adaptation. Creating a sequel to a video game or a remix of a song is an adaptation. The original author holds the keys to all these derivative works.

The Right of Public Performance: This applies to works like music and plays. A bar or restaurant can't just play any music it wants for its customers without permission. A theater company can't stage a play without securing the performance rights from the playwright.

The Right to Broadcast: This is similar to public performance but covers technologies like radio, television, and, in modern interpretations, internet streaming.

By forcing all member countries to recognize these core economic rights, the Berne Convention ensures that copyright has real, tangible, and commercial value across the globe.

3. The Groundbreaking Moral Rights

Third, and perhaps most revolutionary for its time, the Berne Convention requires the protection of an author's Moral Rights.

These are different from the economic rights. Economic rights are about money and property; they can be bought, sold, and inherited. Moral rights are about honor and artistry. They are personal to the author and, in many legal systems, cannot be sold. Article 6bis of the Convention specifically protects two:

The Right of Paternity (or Attribution): This is the right to be identified as the author of your work. It's the right to "claim authorship." You cannot take a painting, scrub off the artist's signature, and put your own name on it. Even if you legally buy the painting, you don't own the right to claim you created it.

The Right of Integrity: This is the right for an author to object to any distortion, mutilation, or modification of their work that would be "prejudicial to his honor or reputation." This protects the work from being debased. For example, a sculptor could use this right to prevent someone from painting their serious bronze statue a ridiculous color. A film director could object if a studio chopped up their film so badly that it no longer made sense and damaged their artistic reputation.

By including moral rights, Berne recognized that creative work is not just a piece of property; it's an extension of the author's personality and reputation.

4. A Minimum Duration of Protection

Finally, the Berne Convention sets a minimum time limit for how long this protection must last. This ensures that a work doesn't fall into the public domain in one country while it's still protected in another.

The general rule is a "floor" of life of the author plus 50 years after their death (often abbreviated pma, or post mortem auctoris).

This means the creator is protected for their entire life. After they die, their family, their estate, or whoever inherits their copyright gets to control and benefit from the work for another 50 years. This allows creators to provide a legacy for their heirs.

Again, this is a minimum. Member countries are free to offer longer terms, and many do. The United States and the entire European Union, for instance, have extended this term to life of the author plus 70 years. This is perfectly compatible with Berne because "life + 70" is more protection than the "life + 50" floor. This long, harmonized duration provides predictability and stability for the global trade in creative works.

Sub-topic 2.3: The WIPO Copyright Treaty (WCT) and the Digital Agenda

The 1990s were not just a new decade; they were the dawn of a new world. The hum of dial-up modems was the soundtrack to a revolution. For the first time, information wasn't just physical. It was becoming a "file." Music, articles, photos, and even movies could be digitized, compressed, and, most terrifyingly for creators, perfectly copied and shared with millions of people at almost no cost.

This was the profound challenge facing the global copyright system. The Berne Convention, our foundational copyright treaty from 1886, was built for an analog world—a world of printing presses, bookstores, and radio broadcasts. It spoke of "reproduction" in terms of physical copies. It had no concept of an MP3, a peer-to-peer network, or a website that could deliver a novel to a computer screen in seconds.

The entire copyright framework was at risk of becoming irrelevant. In response, the global community convened at the World Intellectual Property Organization (WIPO) in Geneva. The result, in 1996, was the WIPO Copyright Treaty (WCT), a document so central to our modern online life that it's often called the "Internet Treaty."

The WCT was a clever piece of legal work. It didn't throw the Berne Convention away. Instead, it acted as a "special agreement" under Berne, like a modern software patch for a classic operating system. Its goal was to clarify, update, and add crucial new components to make copyright functional in the age of the internet.

Clarifying Old Rights for a New World

First, the WCT made it clear that old rights still applied. A key debate was: if you load a webpage or download a song, is that "reproduction"? The file only exists temporarily in your computer's RAM. The WCT shut down this debate. It confirmed that storing a work in any digital medium, even temporarily, is indeed an act of reproduction. This was a critical first step.

But the treaty's most significant addition was a new, broad right designed specifically for the internet: the right of "communication to the public." This right included a revolutionary new idea—the "making available" right.

Let's break this down, because it's the legal basis for everything from Spotify to Netflix.

Before the WCT, "communication" was mostly about "push" media. A radio station broadcasts a song at 9 PM, and everyone has to listen at 9 PM. The broadcaster was in control.

The internet, however, is a "pull" medium. A website doesn't push an ebook to you. It "makes it available," and you, the user, decide to access it "from a place and at a time individually chosen" by you. This on-demand, interactive nature was new. The WCT's "making available" language was crafted precisely to cover this new reality. It gave creators the exclusive right to decide if and how their work would be placed online for on-demand access.

The "Technological Adjuncts": Digital Locks and Labels

The WCT's authors knew that just creating a new right wasn't enough. On the internet, it's incredibly easy to bypass a "Do Not Copy" sign. So, the treaty introduced two powerful new concepts, often called "technological adjuncts" to copyright. These were practical tools to help enforce the law.

1. Technological Protection Measures (TPMs)

This is the big one. Rights holders were already using technology to protect their work. This technology is known as "digital locks" or, more formally, Digital Rights Management (DRM). Think of the encryption on a DVD that stops you from copying it, the password on a paid PDF, or the code that prevents a video game from being played until its official release date.

The WCT required all member countries to pass laws that protected these locks. It obligated them to provide "adequate legal protection and effective legal remedies against the circumvention" of these TPMs.

This "anti-circumvention" provision was, and remains, incredibly controversial. It effectively created a new law: it became illegal to break a digital lock, even if your reason for breaking it was perfectly legal.

For example, a film critic might need to copy a 30-second clip from a DVD to use in a video review—a classic case of "fair use" or "fair dealing." But to get that clip, they first have to break the DVD's encryption. Under laws passed to implement the WCT (like the U.S. Digital Millennium Copyright Act, or DMCA), the act of breaking the lock is illegal, regardless of the "fair" intent.

This has had massive ripple effects. It has been criticized for stifling security research (researchers who discover flaws in DRM can be threatened with lawsuits), hindering archival (libraries can't preserve software or games if they're locked by DRM), and blocking access for people with disabilities (a locked ebook might not work with a screen reader).

2. Rights Management Information (RMI)

This second adjunct was less controversial but just as important. RMI is the digital "label" or "tag" attached to a work. This is the metadata that identifies the work, its author, the copyright owner, and the terms of use. It's the EXIF data in a photograph that says who took it, or the ID3 tag in an MP3 file that lists the artist and album.

The WCT made it illegal to intentionally remove or alter this information. Why? Because RMI is crucial for a functioning digital marketplace. If you're a blogger and you find a photo online, you need that RMI to know who to contact for a license. If a musician's name is stripped from their song file, how can they be identified and paid royalties?

By protecting RMI, the WCT aimed to prevent the creation of "orphan works"—millions of digital files floating on the internet with no owner, making licensing impossible and creativity a free-for-all.

In summary, the WCT was the bridge that carried 19th-century copyright law into the 21st century. It confirmed that digital copies were still copies, created a new right to control on-demand access, and gave rights holders new legal tools (and new controversies) in the form of protected digital locks and labels.

Sub-topic 2.4: The Berne Three-Step Test: A Global Framework for Copyright Exceptions

Copyright has never been a one-way street. It's not an absolute, god-given right of total control. From its very beginning, copyright has always been a balance. It's a bargain between creators and the public. In exchange for a temporary monopoly (the exclusive rights), the public eventually gets the work in the public domain. And even during the copyright term, the public retains the right to make certain uses of the work without permission.

These "safety valves" are called limitations and exceptions. They are the breathing room in the system. They ensure that copyright doesn't stifle the very creativity it's supposed to promote. Exceptions are what allow a book reviewer to quote a passage, a comedian to parody a song, a teacher to photocopy a poem for class, or a library to preserve a fragile book.

But if every country created its own wild exceptions, the global system would fall apart. An exception "for any educational use" in one country could destroy the market for textbooks from another.

The Berne Convention needed a universal standard—a common framework to guide national lawmakers. It needed a "ruler" to measure whether an exception was fair and balanced. This ruler is the Berne Three-Step Test.

First introduced in a limited way in 1967 (in Article 9(2), applying only to the right of reproduction), this test was so useful that its scope was massively expanded. The TRIPS Agreement and the WCT later applied it to all exclusive rights. Today, it is the single most important legal test in international copyright law.

The test is a cumulative, three-part filter. To be valid, a new copyright exception proposed by a national legislature must pass through all three of these gates.

1. The First Step: "Certain Special Cases"

The first gate is about clarity and scope. The exception must be "confined to 'certain special cases.'"

This means the exception must be clearly defined and narrow. It can't be a vague, open-ended free-for-all. For example, an exception that says "any non-commercial use is fine" would be far too broad. It's not "special"; it's a giant hole in the law.

A "special case" is one with a specific, articulated purpose.

Good example: "An exception to allow public libraries to make a single digital copy of a fragile book for archival preservation purposes." This is special and clear.

Good example: "An exception to allow the use of short quotations from a work for the purpose of criticism or review." This is a well-defined case.

Bad example: "An exception for uses that are 'fair.'" This is too general.

This step ensures that lawmakers are deliberate. They can't just wave their hand and create a massive exemption. They must target a specific public policy goal.

2. The Second Step: "Not Conflict with a Normal Exploitation of the Work"

This is the economic heart of the test. Once an exception is defined as a "special case," it must be checked against the marketplace. It must "not conflict with a normal exploitation of the work."

"Normal exploitation" means the primary ways a creator makes money from their work. For a filmmaker, it's selling tickets, streaming rights, and selling Blu-rays. For a novelist, it's selling books (hardcover, paperback, and ebook). For a musician, it's streaming royalties, album sales, and public performance (radio) licenses.

An exception "conflicts" with this if it directly replaces or usurps one of those markets. It's a test of direct economic competition.

Let's use the example from your text:

A law allowing a library to make a single photocopy of a journal article for a student's private research. Does this pass? Probably. The student is not a market; they were unlikely to buy the entire journal for one article. This doesn't replace a "normal exploitation."

A law allowing a university to digitize its entire collection of in-copyright textbooks and put them on the campus network for free. Does this pass? Absolutely not. This directly conflicts with the "normal exploitation" of those works, which is selling textbooks to students. The exception becomes a direct market substitute, and it fails this step.

This step is about protecting the current and potential markets for a work.

3. The Third Step: "Not Unreasonably Prejudice the Legitimate Interests of the Author"

This is the final backstop. Even if an exception is a "special case" (Step 1) and doesn't seem to compete with a normal market (Step 2), it might still be fundamentally unfair. This third step looks at the total harm done to the creator.

The key phrase here is "legitimate interests." This includes more than just money. It also includes the author's moral rights—the right to be named as the author (attribution) and the right to object to a distortion or mutilation of their work (integrity).

An exception might not hurt sales, but it could still "unreasonably prejudice" the author. Imagine a law that allows a political group to take any song, rewrite the lyrics to be hateful, and perform it at rallies, all without permission. This might pass Step 2 (it's not a "normal" market for the musician), but it would almost certainly fail Step 3. It causes an unreasonable level of harm (prejudice) to the author's legitimate interest in not having their work associated with a hateful message.

The other key word is "unreasonably." The test doesn't say "no prejudice." Any exception will cause some small prejudice. That's the point. But it must not be unreasonable. It's a balancing act. A small harm to the creator for a large public benefit (like disability access) might be reasonable. A large harm for a trivial benefit would not.

Together, these three steps form a flexible but disciplined framework. They empower countries to create new exceptions for new technologies (like temporary caching by search engines) but force them to do so in a way that respects the fundamental rights of creators. It is the critical, globally-accepted tool for maintaining the delicate balance between protecting creators and promoting access to culture and information for all.

The Author's Bundle of Rights: Economic and Moral Prerogatives

The Author's Bundle: More Than Just Property

When we talk about "copyright," it's easy to think of it as a single "Keep Out" sign that an author hangs on their work. But the reality is far more complex and fascinating. Copyright isn't one right; it's a bundle of rights. Think of it less like a single key and more like a janitor's keyring, holding many different keys that each unlock a different door. The law gives this entire keyring to the creator of a work, like a novel, a song, or a painting.

These rights are "severable," which is a legal-sounding word for a simple idea: you can give one key to one person and another key to someone else, all while still being the owner of the keyring.

This bundle is split into two very different categories: Economic Rights and Moral Rights. Understanding this split is the most important step in understanding an author's power.

Economic Rights are exactly what they sound like: they're about the money. They are the "proprietary" part of copyright, meaning they can be treated like property. You can sell them, license them, rent them, or even give them away. These are the rights that make publishing a business. When an author "sells their book" to a publisher, they are almost never selling the entire copyright. Instead, they are licensing (or temporarily "renting") specific economic rights—like the right to print and sell the book in English in North America—for a certain number of years.

Moral Rights, on the other hand, are not about money. They are about the author's personal connection to their work. They protect the author's reputation and legacy. These rights are not "property" in the same way; they are personal. In many countries, especially in Europe under systems like the French droit moral, these rights are considered so personal that an author cannot sell them, even if they want to. They stick with the author for life, and sometimes even pass to their heirs.

There are two main moral rights:

The Right of Paternity (or Attribution): This is the right to be named as the author of your work. It's the right to have your name on the cover of your book. It also includes the right to not be named, meaning you can publish anonymously or under a pseudonym.

The Right of Integrity: This is the right to prevent your work from being subjected to "derogatory treatment." This means you can object to any distortion, mutilation, or modification of your work that harms your personal honor or reputation. For example, if someone bought your serious, dramatic novel and published a version of it with a new, silly ending that made the entire story a joke, you could potentially invoke your right of integrity to stop them.

It's important to know that the United States has a very weak system for moral rights compared to the rest of the world. U.S. law is almost entirely focused on the economic side. The main moral rights law in the U.S., the Visual Artists Rights Act (VARA), protects only certain types of visual art, like paintings and sculptures. It specifically excludes literary works, movies, and electronic publications. For authors of books, the main protection for their "integrity" often comes from contract law or unfair competition laws, not a pure moral right.

So, while the economic rights are the engine of the creative industry, the moral rights are its soul, protecting the personal link between a creator and what they created.

Sub-topic 3.1: The Core Economic Rights: Reproduction, Distribution, and Adaptation

These three rights are the bread and butter of the publishing world. They are the "core" economic rights that an author and publisher negotiate over.

The Right of Reproduction

This is the most basic right of all. It is the exclusive right to make copies of the work.

In the old days, this was simple. It meant the right to run a printing press and print physical books. If a publisher wanted to print 5,000 hardcover copies, they needed the author's permission (a license) for the reproduction of those 5,000 copies.

But in the digital age, this right has become incredibly complex. What is a "copy"? The law says a copy is made when a work is "fixed" in any material form, even for a short time. This has huge consequences.

When you buy an ebook, a new digital file is reproduced on your Kindle or computer. That's a reproduction. When you stream an audiobook, a temporary copy of the audio file is created in your computer's memory (its RAM) to allow for smooth playback. Even that temporary "RAM copy," which might vanish a second later, is legally considered a reproduction.

This means the right of reproduction is implicated in almost every single thing we do with digital media. An author who controls this right controls not just the printing of their book, but also its ability to be emailed, downloaded, saved to a hard drive, or even streamed online. It's the foundational "on-off" switch for a work's existence in the market.

The Right of Distribution

This right is the natural partner to reproduction. It's not enough to just make copies; you need the right to give or sell those copies to the public. This right governs how a book gets from the warehouse to the reader.

This right covers shipping books to Amazon, stocking them on the shelves at Barnes & Noble, and, crucially, selling the digital file on an ebook platform.

However, this right has a very famous and important limit: the First Sale Doctrine (also called "exhaustion"). This doctrine says that once the copyright owner (the author or publisher) sells a physical copy of a work, their control over the distribution of that specific copy is "exhausted."

In simple terms: when you buy a new hardcover book, you own the physical object. You don't own the copyright (the story, the text), but you own the paper and glue. Because you own that object, you can do what you want with it. You can sell it to a used bookstore. You can lend it to a friend. You can donate it to a library. The publisher can't stop you. That's the first sale doctrine in action.

This is where the biggest battle in modern copyright is being fought. The first sale doctrine only applies to physical copies. It does not apply to digital works like ebooks. Why? Because you don't "buy" an ebook. You license it. You are buying permission to read the file, but you don't own it.

That's why your ebook license agreement says you can't transfer or resell it.

When you "resell" a digital file, you're not giving someone your original file (like a physical book); you're just making a perfect new copy for them. As a famous court case (Capitol Records v. ReDigi) decided, this "resale" infringes the reproduction right, so the first sale doctrine doesn't even come into play. This is the single biggest difference between owning a physical library and a digital one.

The Right to Create Derivative Works (Adaptation)

This is often the most valuable right in the entire bundle. It is the exclusive right to create a new work based on the original work. This is the "franchise" right.

A derivative work, or adaptation, takes the creative expression from the original work and recasts, transforms, or adapts it into a new form. The provided examples are perfect:

A translation of a novel into Spanish.

An audiobook version.

A film or television series based on the book.

A stage play.

Other examples include abridged versions, prequels, sequels (if not written by the original author), and even study guides. The new work (the movie) gets its own copyright, but it is a derivative copyright that depends on the permission of the original work (the novel).

This right is what allows an author to sell their "film rights" to a Hollywood studio for a large sum, while separately selling their "English language print rights" to a publisher. They are slicing up the bundle.

It's important to distinguish an adaptation from a transformative fair use. A film adaptation "supersedes" the original's market (you watch the movie instead of reading the book for that experience). A parody or a critical review, however, might use parts of the original but for a different purpose—to comment on it or critique it. This "transformative use" is often protected as fair use and does not require a license, creating another complex but important line in copyright law.

Sub-topic 3.2: The Public-Facing Economic Rights: Public Performance and Display

These last two economic rights are less about making and selling copies and more about controlling how the work is experienced in public.

The Right of Public Performance

This is the exclusive right to perform the work publicly. For a literary work, "perform" means to recite it aloud.

What does "publicly" mean? The law has a two-part definition. A performance is public if it happens:

At a place open to the public (like a park, a bookstore, or a theater).

At any place where a "substantial number of persons" outside a normal family circle is gathered (like a private club, a school, or a corporate meeting).

This right also, and most importantly, covers transmitting the performance to the public. This means the public doesn't have to be in the same room. Broadcasting an audiobook over the radio is a public performance. Streaming an audiobook on a service like Audible is a public performance (even if everyone listens at a different time).

A live poetry reading at a coffee shop is a public performance. A professional storyteller reciting a chapter of a book on stage is a public performance. A high school putting on a performance of a play requires a public performance license.

This right also has important exceptions. The most common one for literary works is the "face-to-face teaching" exception. A teacher at a non-profit school is allowed to read a poem or a section of a novel aloud to their students in a physical classroom as part of a lesson. This is not considered an infringement. However, this exception is narrow. It would not cover that same teacher posting a video of themselves reading the chapter to the open internet or using it in a for-profit online course.

The Right of Public Display

Finally, we have the right of public display. This right is often confused with performance, but the difference is simple: a performance is sequential (it happens over time, like reading a story), while a display is static (you show one thing).

The right of public display is the exclusive right to show a copy of the work to the public. For visual art, this is obvious: it's the right to hang a painting in a public gallery.

For a literary work, this right is a bit more abstract but just as important in the digital age. Projecting a page of a novel onto a screen during a public lecture is a public display. Displaying the text of a poem on a public website is a public display.

Think about the "Look Inside" feature on Amazon. That is a licensed use of the public display right. The publisher has given Amazon permission to display a certain number of pages to the public for marketing. If you did the same thing on your personal blog without permission—scanned and posted the first chapter for everyone to see—you would be infringing both the reproduction right (by scanning it) and the public display right (by posting it).

Like the performance right, the first sale doctrine creates a small exception here. The owner of a particular physical copy is allowed to display that one copy publicly. This is why a bookstore can put a book in its front window. They own that copy. But they cannot scan the cover and display it on their website without a license, as that would be a new display of a reproduction, not a display of the original physical object.

Sub-topic 3.3: Moral Rights (Droit Moral): The Right of Attribution (Paternity)

When an author creates a novel, a songwriter pens a lyric, or an artist paints a canvas, they create more than just a piece of property. They create something that is uniquely tied to them, a piece of their own personality and intellect given form. While most of copyright law focuses on the economic side of this creation—the right to copy, sell, and profit—there is a whole other category of rights that protects this personal link. These are known as "moral rights," or droit moral in French, where the concept was first given its strongest voice.

This idea comes from the civil law tradition, common in continental Europe. This system views an author's work as a direct extension of their personality. It's not just a product they made; it's a part of who they are. Because this link is so personal, the law believes it deserves special protection, separate from the right to make money.

The most important international treaty on copyright, the Berne Convention, recognizes this. It requires all its member countries—over 180 of them, including the United States—to protect at least two fundamental moral rights. These rights are laid out in Article 6bis of the convention.

The first and most fundamental of these is the right of attribution, also known as the right of paternity.

At its core, this right is simple: it is the author's right to be identified as the creator of their work. Think of it as the right to "sign your name." The term "paternity" is very descriptive; it frames the author as the "parent" of the work. This right ensures that an author receives the credit they are due and, just as importantly, prevents others from falsely claiming authorship and stealing that credit.

However, the right of attribution is a two-sided coin. It also includes the vital, correlative right to control how you are named. This means an author has the right to publish a work anonymously. If they fear political persecution for their writing, or simply wish for privacy, they can choose to publish with no name attached. Similarly, they have the right to publish under a pseudonym, a false name. Think of writers like Mark Twain (Samuel Clemens) or George Eliot (Mary Ann Evans). The right of attribution protects their choice to use that pen name, or to remain anonymous entirely. It is about controlling the public link between the author and the work.

This is where the world of law splits into two very different paths. The strength and nature of this right change dramatically depending on the legal system you are in.

In civil law countries like France and Germany, the right of attribution is a core principle. It is considered a fundamental, inalienable, and often perpetual right. Let's break those words down.

Fundamental: It is a basic right of being a creator, like a human right for authors.

Inalienable: This is the most crucial part. It means the author cannot permanently sell or give away this right. Even if a publisher offers them a million dollars to sign a contract waiving their right to be named, that part of the contract is often considered void. The personal link to the work cannot be broken by a simple business transaction.

Perpetual: In many of these systems, the right lasts forever, or at least as long as the economic rights (which can be 70+ years after the author's death). Their heirs can continue to insist that the creator's name be properly attributed.

Now, let's cross the ocean to common law systems like the United States. The situation is completely different.

For a long time, the U.S. legal system was almost hostile to the idea of moral rights. The focus was always on the economic bargain. The U.S. only formally adopted moral rights when it joined the Berne Convention. To do so, it passed the Visual Artists Rights Act (VARA) in 1990.

But VARA is extremely narrow. It applies only to a small category of visual art—things like paintings, drawings, prints, or sculptures that exist in a single copy or in a limited edition of 200 or fewer copies.

VARA explicitly excludes literary works. It does not apply to novels, poems, screenplays, musical compositions, or journalistic articles.

So, for an American author, where does the right to be named on the cover of their book come from? It comes from one place: the contract.

The right of attribution in the U.S. is not an inherent, statutory moral right for most authors. It is a right that must be negotiated with the publisher and written into the publishing agreement. If the contract says the publisher must put the author's name on the cover, they must. If it doesn't, they are under no statutory obligation to do so (though it would be a very strange business practice not to). This transforms the right from a matter of personal honor into a simple, negotiable term of a business deal.

This weakness was confirmed in a major Supreme Court case, Dastar Corp. v. Twentieth Century Fox Film Corp. (2003). In that case, a company took an old TV series whose copyright had expired, edited it slightly, and sold it on DVD as its own product, with no mention of the original creators. The original creators sued under trademark law (the Lanham Act), claiming this was "false designation of origin." The Supreme Court disagreed, ruling that the Lanham Act was intended to protect the origin of physical goods (the company that made the DVD), not the creative ideas within those goods. This was a significant blow, making it very difficult for U.S. authors to use trademark law to enforce their right of attribution.

Other common law countries have found a middle ground. The United Kingdom, for example, has stronger protections in its Copyright, Designs and Patents Act 1988. This law does give literary authors a statutory right to be identified. However, unlike in France, this right is not automatic. The author must formally "assert" it in writing (like in their contract). It can also be "waived" in a contract. This makes it much stronger than the U.S. system, but still weaker than the inalienable right found in the civil law tradition.

Ultimately, the right to "sign your name" seems simple. But in the eyes of the law, it reveals a profound philosophical divide about what it means to be an author: a parent with an unbreakable personal bond to their creation, or a producer who has made a product to be sold.

Sub-topic 3.4: Moral Rights (Droit Moral): The Right of Integrity

If the right of attribution protects the link between the creator and the work, the right of integrity protects the work itself from being dishonored. It is the second core moral right mandated by the Berne Convention.

Article 6bis grants the author the right to object to any "distortion, mutilation or other modification of, or other derogatory action in relation to, the said work, which would be prejudicial to his honor or reputation."

This language is very specific and important. This right is not about preventing any and all changes. It doesn't stop a book from being translated, a novel from being adapted into a movie, or a song from being remixed (though other rights might). It is about protecting the work from alterations that would harm the author's reputation by misrepresenting their creation. It's about preventing changes that make the author look bad or twist their original message into something it was not.

The key phrase is "prejudicial to his honor or reputation." The author must prove that the change isn't just a change; it's a harmful one that damages their public standing as a creative professional.

Just like with attribution, the application of this right differs starkly across jurisdictions.

In France, the right of integrity is robust and treated with utmost seriousness. It is also perpetual, meaning an author's heirs can defend the work's integrity long after the author is gone. For example, an author's estate could sue to stop a film adaptation that they feel fundamentally betrays the spirit of the original novel. In a famous case, the heirs of the author Victor Hugo successfully sued to stop a movie adaptation of Les Misérables that they felt distorted the work. This right is a powerful tool to ensure that the work, as an extension of the author's personality, is not disrespected.

Now, let's return to the United States. As we saw, the main federal statute for moral rights, VARA, is limited to a narrow category of visual artists. For those specific artists, the right of integrity is protected. An artist whose painting is intentionally distorted or mutilated in a way that harms their reputation can sue for damages.

But what about everyone else? What about authors, screenwriters, composers, and filmmakers? They are not covered by VARA. For decades, this left them with almost no legal protection if their work was butchered by a studio or publisher.

This exact problem led to one of the most famous and creative U.S. cases on the subject: Gilliam v. American Broadcasting Companies (1976).

The members of the British comedy troupe Monty Python had sold the rights for their television programs, "Monty Python's Flying Circus," to the ABC network. ABC, in order to fit the shows into a standard time slot with commercials, proceeded to heavily edit them. They cut out 24 minutes from a 90-minute special, removing essential jokes, disrupting the comedic flow, and fundamentally altering the creative product.

The Pythons were horrified. They felt this edited version was a "mutilation" that made their carefully crafted work look disjointed and unfunny. They argued this was deeply prejudicial to their honor and reputation as comedians.

However, they were in the U.S. They couldn't sue under a "moral right of integrity" because, for a television program, no such right existed in U.S. law. So, their lawyers had to find another way.

They used a legal principle from trademark and unfair competition law, Section 43(a) of the Lanham Act. This law prevents "false designation of origin" or "false representations" in commerce.

The Pythons' argument was brilliant. They claimed that by broadcasting this mangled, distorted version of their show under the Monty Python name, ABC was lying to the public. They were presenting a work that was not the real Monty Python creation and passing it off as the genuine article. The court compared it to taking a famous artist's painting, cropping it, repainting parts of it, and then still selling it as the original artist's work.

The court agreed. It found that ABC's edits were so severe that they amounted to a "mutilation" of the work. By presenting this distorted version to the public under the

Monty Python name, ABC had created a false attribution, which was actionable under the Lanham Act.

The Gilliam case is a landmark because it shows how, in the absence of a strong statutory moral right, U.S. courts have sometimes used legal detours to protect an author's right of integrity. It's a "hack" that uses principles of false advertising to achieve what droit moral does directly.

This issue continues to be relevant today, especially in the digital age. What about the "colorization" of old black-and-white films, which many directors argued was a mutilation of their artistic choices? What about "clean" versions of films, where a third-party company edits out violence or profanity against the director's wishes? What about AI-powered tools that can alter a digital painting, or remix a song in a way the original artist finds offensive?

The right of integrity sits at the heart of a difficult tension. It tries to protect an author's vision, but it can clash with the rights of the person who now owns the physical work, as well as the rights of others to comment on, parody, or transform that work. In the end, it's a legal system's attempt to answer a very human question: How much control does a creator get to keep over their work after they've released it to the world?

Part II: Securing and Managing Copyright

The Automatic Shield: Copyright Protection upon Creation

4.1: The Principle of Automatic Protection Explained

Imagine you're sitting in a café. You pull out a notebook and, inspired, you write a short poem. Or perhaps you're a musician, and you hum a new melody into your phone's voice recorder. Maybe you're a designer, and you sketch a logo on a napkin. In that exact instant—the second the ink dries, the digital file is saved, the soundwave is captured—you have created a copyright.

You didn't fill out a form. You didn't mail anything to a government office. You didn't pay a fee.

This is the single most important and often misunderstood concept in all of copyright law: protection is automatic. It is a fundamental, global right that springs into existence with the very act of creation. It's not something you have to "get." It's something you have, immediately and without cost.

This powerful global standard is the cornerstone of the modern international copyright system. Its legal backbone is a treaty called the Berne Convention for the Protection of Literary and Artistic Works. This agreement, which has been signed by over 180 countries, sets a minimum standard of protection for creators. And its most crucial mandate is that copyright protection cannot be dependent on any "formality."

What does this mean, "no formality"? It means countries that sign the treaty agree to throw out all the old, bureaucratic hoops that creators used to have to jump through. In the past, you might have had to publish your work, or put a special notice on it, or register it with a national office just to claim it was yours. The Berne Convention abolished all of that. It leveled the playing field, ensuring that a poet in a small village has the same immediate protection as a massive publishing house in a major city.

The only requirement, the single trigger for this automatic shield, is a concept called "fixation."

A work must be "fixed in a tangible medium of expression." This sounds like complex legal jargon, but it's incredibly simple. It just means the work has to be recorded in some way that is stable and can be perceived or reproduced. It must be moved from a pure idea into a form.

Copyright does not protect ideas. You cannot copyright the idea of a boy wizard who goes to a magic school, or the idea of a tragic romance between families at war. But the moment you write a story about a specific wizard named Harry Potter, or a play about two specific lovers named Romeo and Juliet, you have "fixed" that idea into a unique expression. That expression is protected.

Fixation is the line in the sand.

Thinking about a song in your head? Not fixed. No copyright.

Singing that song and recording it on your laptop? It is now fixed. You have a copyright in that recording and the underlying musical work.

Having an idea for a painting? Not fixed.

Applying paint to a canvas to create that painting? It is fixed. You have a copyright.

Saving a document on your computer, writing in a journal, taking a photograph, or sculpting a piece of clay—all of these are acts of fixation.

This principle isn't just a theory; it is the law of the land in major jurisdictions across the globe. The United Kingdom, for example, does not have a government-run register of copyrights. Protection is simply automatic when an original work is created. The same principle holds true in Canada, where your rights are established under both Canadian and international law from the very second of creation.

Look to Australia, and you'll find the same philosophy: copyright protection is described as "free and automatic" from the moment the work is put into a "material form." Across the entire European Union, this standard is universal. Nations like Spain, Germany, and France grant copyright based on the "sole act of creation," with no need for any deposit or registration formalities.

This global harmony provides a powerful, immediate, and reassuring shield for authors, artists, and creators of all kinds. It means your rights are not fragile. They don't depend on a piece of paper in a filing cabinet. Your creative work is born with its own suit of armor, established the instant you save the file, snap the photo, or write the final word. This understanding is the first and most critical step in managing your creative assets.

4.2: The Role and Proper Use of the Copyright Notice (©)

If copyright protection is truly automatic from the moment of creation, it begs a very logical question: Why does everyone still use the little © symbol?

It's one of the most recognizable symbols in the world, appearing on books, movies, websites, and album covers. Its persistence creates a common point of confusion, leading many to believe it's a legal requirement. For a long time, in some places, it was.

The answer lies in a major historical shift, particularly in the United States. Before March 1, 1989, U.S. law was different. To secure and maintain copyright for any work that was "published" (made available to the public), the U.S. required the use of a proper copyright notice. If an author published a book and forgot to include the notice, or formatted it incorrectly, the consequences could be catastrophic. The work could be irreversibly injected into the public domain, all rights lost forever.

Everything changed in 1989. This was the year the United States fully joined the Berne Convention. To align its laws with the rest of the world and adopt the "automatic protection" principle, Congress had to abolish the mandatory notice.

Since that date, the copyright notice has been legally optional in the United States, just as it is in most of the world. You do not need it for your copyright to exist. You will not lose your rights if you forget to add it. Your work is protected from the moment of fixation, period.

So, we return to the question: If it's not required, why bother?

The answer is that while the notice has lost its foundational legal power, it has retained enormous practical and strategic power. Using it is no longer a legal necessity, but it remains a highly recommended best practice. Think of it less as the shield itself (fixation is the shield) and more as a bright, clear label painted on the shield, warning everyone that it exists and telling them who holds it.

There are several strategic reasons to use it.

First, it serves as a clear public declaration of your rights. It's a "No Trespassing" sign for your intellectual property. It instantly dispels any ambiguity. It tells the world, "This is not in the public domain. Someone owns this, and they are aware of their rights." This simple act can deter a huge amount of casual, opportunistic infringement. An amateur blogger looking for an image is far more likely to skip over the one with a clear copyright notice and look for one that appears to be "free."

Second, it identifies the owner and simplifies licensing. The notice acts like a business card for your work. If a filmmaker, publisher, or marketing agency wants to legitimately license your photograph, song, or article, the notice tells them exactly who to contact. Without it, they may not know where to even begin seeking permission, and a potential licensing opportunity could be lost.

Third, and perhaps most importantly in the U.S., it provides a powerful legal weapon in court. In the United States, an infringer might try to lessen their financial penalty by claiming "innocent infringement." They might argue, "I had no idea this was copyrighted! I found it on the internet; I thought it was free to use." This defense, if successful, can significantly reduce the "statutory damages" a court will award.

A proper copyright notice makes this entire defense evaporate. The law is clear: if a proper notice is present on the work, no court will accept a defense of "innocent infringement." The infringer is considered to be on notice, and they are fully liable. This single benefit can be worth thousands, or even tens of thousands, of dollars in a legal dispute.

Given these benefits, adding a notice is a low-cost, high-impact tool. And fortunately, formatting it is extremely simple. A proper notice consists of three parts, in any order:

The Symbol: The © (the letter C in a circle) is the most recognized international symbol. You can also use the word "Copyright" or the abbreviation "Copr."

The Year of First Publication: This is the year you first made the work available to the public. If the work is updated over time (like a website or a software program), you might see a range (e.g., "© 2018-2025").

The Name of the Copyright Owner: This can be the author's real name, a pen name, or the name of the company that owns the copyright.

A perfect, simple example would be: © 2025 Jane Doe

This simple line, typically placed on the copyright page of a book, in the footer of a website, or on the back of a print, is one of the easiest and most effective things a creator can do to assert their ownership and protect their work in the marketplace.

4.3 Establishing a "Poor Man's Copyright": Myth vs. Reality

In the creative world, few ideas are as persistent, as appealing, and as dangerously wrong as the "poor man's copyright." It's a piece of folklore, passed down from one generation of writers, musicians, and artists to the next. The process sounds so simple and clever. You finish your manuscript, your song, or your design. You print a copy, put it in a sturdy envelope, and take it to the post office. You pay for registered or certified mail and send it directly back to yourself.

When it arrives, you don't open it. You store it away in a file cabinet or a desk drawer, a "legal time capsule" sealed with an official, government-issued postmark. In your mind, you've just created a perfect, inexpensive piece of evidence. You've "proven" the date your creation existed, ready to be unveiled in a courtroom to defeat any thief who claims your work as their own.

Unfortunately, this entire practice is legally worthless. It is a myth. Relying on it is the equivalent of building a firewall out of paper. It provides a false, and incredibly dangerous, sense of security.

Let's be perfectly clear: In the United States, and in most countries, this method provides absolutely no substitute for formal registration with a national copyright office. The U.S. Copyright Office has been very direct about this. For decades, they have explicitly stated that the "poor man's copyright" is not a substitute for registration. It is not recognized in the law, and it does not grant you any of the powerful legal benefits that formal registration does.

The core problem is one of evidence. In a legal dispute, a self-addressed, sealed envelope carries almost no evidentiary weight. Imagine the scene in a real courtroom. You are suing someone for infringement. Your lawyer presents the unopened envelope to the judge. The opposing lawyer would immediately, and rightly, object.

What would their argument be? It would be simple and devastating.

First, they would argue that the contents are unverifiable. How does the court really know what is inside that envelope? Even if you open it in front of the judge, how do they know that is the original, unaltered manuscript?

Second, they would argue that the envelope is not tamper-proof. An envelope can be carefully steamed open, its contents swapped out, and then resealed. A skilled individual could do this without leaving obvious evidence. The opposing counsel would suggest that you could have mailed yourself an empty envelope (or an old phone bill) in 2023, and then, after discovering the defendant's work in 2025, steamed it open, inserted your infringing copy, and sealed it back up. It sounds like a conspiracy, but the possibility of it is enough to create reasonable doubt.

Third, and most importantly, it does not create a public record of your claim. This is the entire point of a government copyright office. When you register your work, you are making a formal, public declaration. Your claim is entered into a searchable, national database. This "puts the world on notice" that you are the claimant. Your mailed envelope is a private act. It notifies no one. The legal system is built on public, verifiable records, not private, sealed-away acts of faith.

This myth likely started in an era before digital technology. Decades ago, before computers with metadata, before email servers with third-party timestamps, and before cloud-based version history, creators struggled with how to prove when they created something. Mailing a copy seemed like a plausible, low-tech hack. But today, even without registration, you have far better options. A saved file on your computer has metadata. An email you sent to a friend or an agent with the manuscript attached is a much stronger piece of evidence, as it's held by a neutral third party (like Google or Microsoft) and has a timestamp that is extremely difficult to fake.

The real danger of the "poor man's copyright" is not just that it doesn't work. The danger is that it actively discourages creators from doing the one thing that does work: formally registering their copyright. A creator who trusts that sealed envelope in their desk drawer feels safe. They feel protected. They are not.

When a real infringement dispute happens, that false sense of security vanishes. Their "evidence" is dismissed by the court, and they are left with a weak case, or no case at all. They are left vulnerable, exposed, and full of regret for trusting a clever-sounding but hollow piece of legal folklore. The only legally recognized method for creating a powerful, official record of a copyright claim in the United States is to register the work with the U.S. Copyright Office. Everything else is a gamble.

4.4 Proving Ownership Without Registration: The Evidentiary Challenge

One of the best, and most confusing, things about modern copyright law is that protection is automatic. The moment you write your sentence, paint your stroke, or record your melody—the moment your original idea is "fixed in a tangible medium"—it is legally protected by copyright.

You own it. This is a powerful right, guaranteed by international treaties like the Berne Convention.

But this "automatic" protection creates a deep and difficult paradox. While your ownership is automatic, your ability to prove that ownership in a court of law is not.

If someone steals your work, you can't just walk into court and say, "That's mine!" The legal system runs on proof. In an infringement lawsuit, you are the plaintiff. This means the initial burden of proof rests entirely on you. You must first prove to the court's satisfaction that you are the valid owner of the copyright in the work you claim was stolen.

Without a certificate of registration, this task becomes a steep, uphill climb. This is the great evidentiary challenge.

The single most powerful tool in this situation is a timely registration certificate from the U.S. Copyright Office. A certificate of registration, especially one filed before the infringement or within five years of publication, is considered prima facie evidence of your ownership.

This is a critical legal term. Prima facie is Latin for "at first sight" or "on its face." In the courtroom, it means the judge and jury will presume you are the owner, unless the other side can present compelling evidence to prove you are not. In practical terms, it flips the entire script. The burden of proof instantly shifts from you to the person you are accusing. They now have the incredibly difficult job of proving your registration is somehow invalid. This is a massive strategic advantage.

But what if you don't have that certificate? What if you're like most creators and you never got around to registering?

Your case is not automatically lost, but it just became ten times harder and more expensive. You now have to build your case for ownership from the ground up, piece by piece, like assembling a castle from pebbles. You need to gather every scrap of evidence you can find to establish your claim and, crucially, to demonstrate a timeline of creation that predates the infringing work.

What does this "mosaic" of evidence look like?

Dated Drafts: A stack of papers showing the evolution of your manuscript is a start. However, just like the "poor man's copyright," these are susceptible to challenge. An opposing lawyer could ask, "How do we know you didn't just type these up last week and backdate them?"

Digital Version History: This is much stronger. Modern word processing software (like Microsoft Word or Scrivener) and cloud services (like Google Docs) keep a detailed, time-stamped log of changes. It is much harder to fake this metadata. A digital forensics expert could potentially verify these timestamps, creating a credible timeline of your work.

Email Correspondence: This is one of the strongest forms of proof. If you emailed drafts of your manuscript to an editor, an agent, a beta reader, or even a friend, those emails serve as powerful, time-stamped records. They are held by third-party servers (like Google, Yahoo, or Microsoft), which makes them highly credible and verifiable through a legal process.

Witness Testimony: You could call witnesses to testify. Perhaps your spouse saw you working on it every night. Perhaps you read a chapter to your writing group. Perhaps an agent read it and rejected it. This can be effective, but it is also subjective. The other side will try to paint your witnesses as biased, forgetful, or unreliable.

While you can use these methods to build a case, they are all inherently less authoritative than a single, government-issued certificate. A sharp defense attorney can poke holes in every single one of them. They can challenge the integrity of your hard drive. They can question the memory of your witnesses. They can cast doubt on your motives.

This process of "proving" your ownership is a massive drain on your time, energy, and money. It can add an entire, expensive layer of difficulty to an already stressful lawsuit. You could spend tens of thousands of dollars on legal fees and expert witnesses just to get to "square one"—the point you would have started at if you had a registration certificate.

This evidentiary hurdle is, by itself, one of the most compelling reasons for all serious creators to formally register their work. Registration is not just an administrative formality. It is a legal shield and a powerful sword. It's the difference between showing up to a fight with a verified title deed to your land, or showing up with a handful of blurry photos and hoping someone believes you.

Fortifying Your Claim: The Strategic Value of Formal Copyright Registration

Fortifying Your Claim: The Strategic Value of Formal Copyright Registration

It is one of the most widely shared beliefs among creators: "My work is copyrighted the moment I create it." This is, in fact, true. Thanks to an international treaty called the Berne Convention, which the United States joined in 1989, the old requirement of registering a work or even putting a © notice on it just to have a copyright was abolished. Protection is now automatic. This principle is a wonderful thing for artists, authors, and musicians, granting them foundational rights without forcing them to jump through legal hoops.

However, this foundational principle can create a deeply misleading sense of complete security. There is a vast, practical, and often financially painful gap between possessing a right and being able to enforce it. In practice, the ability to effectively defend one's work against theft or misuse often depends entirely on an additional, voluntary step: formal copyright registration with the U.S. Copyright Office.

This chapter argues that registration should be viewed not as a mere legal formality, but as an essential, proactive strategic business decision. It is an investment in the value and defensibility of your creative assets. Particularly in the United States, which retains a unique hybrid of the Berne Convention's automatic protection and its own older, formality-driven laws, timely registration transforms a theoretical right into a powerful, enforceable asset. It is the action that unlocks the most potent legal remedies available to a copyright owner, turning a simple "No

Trespassing" sign into a locked gate with a full security system.

Before the U.S. joined the Berne Convention, its copyright law was all about formalities. You had to register. You had to use the notice. Failure to follow these steps perfectly could cast your work into the public domain, forever unprotected. When the U.S. modernized its law to align with the rest of the world, it couldn't fully let go of its old system. It compromised. It made copyright automatic (as Berne required) but kept registration as the key to unlocking the courthouse doors and the most powerful financial penalties.

This decision created the system we have today. For creators, especially those just starting, this distinction is critical. Believing that "automatic protection" is all you need is like owning a deed to a house but having no key to the front door. When you find a trespasser inside, you can stand on the lawn and wave your deed, but you can't actually get inside to remove them. Registration is the key. It empowers you to act. It signals to the world, and more importantly to the legal system, that you take your intellectual property seriously and have prepared it for defense. It is the mechanism by which a simple creative expression is converted into a fully realized, bankable, and legally formidable asset. This chapter will explore the two most critical reasons why this single step is the most important strategic move a creator can make.

Sub-topic 5.1: Registration as a Prerequisite for Litigation in the U.S.

The single most critical reason for registering a work in the United States is procedural. It is a hard, inflexible rule. For works of U.S. origin, formal registration is a statutory prerequisite to initiating a copyright infringement lawsuit in federal court. This rule is found in Section 411(a) of the U.S. Copyright Act. It states, with very few exceptions, that an author or publisher simply cannot file a complaint for infringement until the U.S. Copyright Office has either issued a registration certificate or has formally refused to register the work.

This requirement acts as a rigid procedural gate, effectively barring the courthouse doors to unregistered U.S. rights holders. An author who discovers a blatant act of piracy—their new novel being sold on a dozen pirate sites, for instance—is legally powerless to stop it through the courts. Before they can even file for an injunction, they must first file an application with the Copyright Office and wait.

This is not a simple "file and sue" process. For years, there was a disagreement among U.S. courts. Some believed you could sue as soon as you applied for registration. Others argued you had to wait for the Copyright Office to act on your application. This question was decisively settled by the U.S. Supreme Court in the 2019 case Fourth Estate Public Benefit Corp. v. Wall-Street.com. The Court ruled unanimously that "registration" means the Copyright Office has fully processed the application and has either granted the registration or refused it. Just applying is not enough.

This creates a significant practical problem: time. Given that standard processing times for a copyright application can take anywhere from three to nine months, or even longer, this mandatory delay can cause significant and often irreversible harm. The infringement is allowed to continue, to spread, and to profit, all while the legitimate author is stuck in an administrative queue. By the time the registration certificate arrives, the infringer may have closed up shop, disappeared with their profits, or caused such widespread market damage that the author's commercial opportunity is lost forever.

It is interesting to note that this procedural gate generally applies only to "United States works." Because of the Berne Convention, a work first published in another member country (like Canada or France) can be defended in U.S. court without a U.S. registration. This creates the strange situation where a French author has an easier time suing in a U.S. court than an American author. This disparity only highlights the importance for domestic creators to overcome this self-imposed legal hurdle.

What if a creator is facing a true emergency? The Copyright Office does provide an option for "special handling," or expedited registration. If an author can prove a compelling need, such as pending litigation or a publishing deadline, they can pay a substantial fee (currently $800) to have their application reviewed within five business days. While this is a crucial escape hatch, it is expensive and reactive. It is a costly solution to a problem that could have been avoided by a proactive, inexpensive standard registration months earlier.

A more streamlined alternative for smaller disputes is the Copyright Claims Board (CCB), a tribunal established in 2022. This "small claims court" for copyright is designed to handle claims up to $30,000 in a faster, more affordable way than federal court. However, even to access this more accessible forum, the rule is similar. The claimant must either have a completed registration certificate or, in a slight relaxation of the Fourth Estate rule, at least have a registration application pending with the Office. Therefore, in every part of the U.S. legal system, from small claims to the Supreme Court, registration is the indispensable key that unlocks the door to enforcement.

Sub-topic 5.2: Unlocking Statutory Damages and Attorney's Fees

Beyond simply getting you into court, timely registration provides access to the most powerful financial remedies under U.S. copyright law: statutory damages and the potential recovery of attorney's fees. This is where the true strategic and economic value of registration is realized. Without these tools, most copyright litigation would be financially impossible for individual creators.

To be eligible for these powerful remedies, the copyright must be registered in a "timely" manner. The law, specifically Section 412 of the Copyright Act, defines this in two ways. The work must be registered either:

Before the infringement commenced; or

Within a three-month grace period after the work's date of first publication.

This provision is of immense strategic importance. Imagine an author finds their book being given away for free on a pirate website. To win a lawsuit, they would normally have to prove "actual damages." This means calculating the exact financial loss they suffered (e.g., lost sales) plus any profits the infringer made. This is incredibly difficult. How can you prove how many people downloaded the book for free instead of buying it? What if the infringer made no profit at all? The author could spend $50,000 on a lawsuit only to be awarded a few hundred dollars in actual damages.

Statutory damages completely bypass this problem. If the registration was timely, the creator does not have to prove any actual financial harm. The law "presumes" harm. It allows a court to award a pre-determined amount for each work infringed. This amount typically ranges from $750 to $30,000 per work. This means if a photographer finds a company used ten of their photos without permission, a court could award up to $300,000, even if the photographer can't prove they lost a single dollar in sales.

Furthermore, if the copyright owner can prove the infringement was "willful"—meaning the infringer knew what they were doing was wrong—a court can increase the award to as much as $150,000 per work. This is the true deterrent. It's the "hammer" that registration gives to a creator.

The second, and equally powerful, remedy is the recovery of attorney's fees. Copyright litigation is notoriously expensive. Legal fees can easily run into the tens or even hundreds of thousands of dollars. This cost is the single biggest barrier to justice for creators. An infringer can simply ignore a cease-and-desist letter from an individual, knowing they likely can't afford the legal fight.

However, if the work was timely registered, the law gives the court the discretion to order the losing infringer to pay the winner's full attorney's fees. This dramatically alters the economic calculus of litigation. It makes it feasible for individual creators to hire a lawyer and pursue a valid claim, knowing that if they win, they won't be bankrupted by their own legal bills. This is what gives a cease-and-desist letter its teeth. The infringer knows that fighting the claim and losing could now cost them not only statutory damages but also the creator's massive legal bill.

This combination of rules effectively creates the "two-tiered" copyright system you mentioned. Many creators, particularly self-publishers and freelancers, believe that because their work is automatically protected by the

Berne Convention, no further action is necessary. They reside in the lower tier. Their rights are theoretical. If they are infringed, their only recourse is to sue for actual damages (which are hard to prove) and to pay for their own lawyers (which is prohibitively expensive).

An infringer, aware of this, can make a cold, calculated risk. They see an unregistered work and know the creator is, for all practical purposes, defenseless. The rights of these unregistered authors, while theoretically valid, become practically unenforceable against determined infringers. This creates a significant strategic disadvantage.

Timely registration elevates an author from this lower tier of theoretical protection to the upper tier of practical, potent enforceability. It transforms their copyright from a paper shield into a steel sword, giving them the power to not only defend their work but to make infringement a costly and losing proposition for thieves.

5.3: Registration as Public Record and Prima Facie Evidence

In the United States, filing for copyright registration is often viewed as a simple administrative task, but this perspective misses its profound strategic power. The act of registration with the U.S. Copyright Office accomplishes two massive goals: it creates an indisputable public record, and it forges a powerful legal weapon known as prima facie evidence. These functions are the bedrock of copyright commerce and enforcement in the U.S.

The Power of the Public Record

First, let's talk about the public record. When you register a work, you are not just getting a certificate; you are creating a permanent, searchable entry in a massive federal database. This record is accessible to anyone, anywhere in the world. This might not sound exciting, but in the business of creativity, this database is a cornerstone of the entire marketplace.

Imagine you're a film producer. You find a brilliant independent novel you want to adapt into a movie. Your first question is, "Who do I pay?" You can't just send a check to the name on the book cover; that person might have sold the rights, or the rights might be held by a publisher, or they may have passed away and the rights are now with their heirs. A quick search of the Copyright Office's public record can answer this. The registration identifies the legal claimant—the owner of the copyright. It provides a clear, verifiable "chain of title," showing who has the legal authority to license or sell the work.

This public notice function is critical for licensing. Foreign publishers, software developers looking to license code, or advertising agencies needing a song for a commercial all rely on this record. It provides certainty. It allows potential licensees to perform their "due diligence," verifying the status of the work and the identity of the owner. This transparency greases the wheels of commerce. It removes the guesswork and a huge amount of the risk, making deals happen faster and more securely.

This record also serves as a potent deterrent. Because the information is public, it's much harder for an infringer to later claim they were "innocent." They can't plausibly argue they had no way of knowing the work was protected or who owned it. The record establishes, for all the world to see, who claims what and when they claimed it. This clarity is invaluable, turning an abstract intellectual right into a tangible, defined, and discoverable public asset.

The "Legal Shield": Prima Facie Evidence

The second function of registration is where the true legal power lies. This is the concept of prima facie evidence, a Latin term meaning "at first face" or "on its face."

Under U.S. law (specifically, 17 U.S.C. § 410(c)), if you register your work before it's published or within five years of its first publication, your registration certificate is automatically considered by the court to be prima facie evidence. This means the court accepts all the key facts stated on that certificate as true, right from the start of a lawsuit.

What facts? Crucial ones:

That your copyright is valid.

That you are the author (or owner).

That the date of creation you listed is correct.

That the work is original and meets the standards for protection.

This single benefit completely flips the script in a courtroom. Think about it. Without this registration, if you sue someone for infringement, the entire burden of proof is on you. You have to stand before a judge and prove every single one of those points. You'd have to dig up old computer files, find early drafts, get witnesses to testify, and build an entire case just to establish that you have a valid copyright before you can even begin to argue that the defendant copied you. It is an expensive, time-consuming, and difficult process.

Now, picture walking into court with a timely registration certificate. You hand it to the judge. Because of the prima facie status, the judge effectively turns to the defendant—the alleged infringer—and says, "The law presumes everything on this certificate is true. The plaintiff owns a valid copyright. Now, it is your job to prove that they don't."

This shift in the burden of proof is a game-changer. The legal presumption of ownership is now on your side. The defendant is immediately on the defensive. They are forced to start the fight from the bottom of a very steep hill.

To win, the defendant must now try to rebut (disprove) the certificate. This is not easy. They can't just claim it's invalid. They have to provide substantial evidence to prove, for example, that you committed fraud on the Copyright Office (by knowingly lying on your application) or that your work completely lacks the originality required for copyright. This is a very high hurdle for a defendant to clear.

This procedural advantage is so powerful that it often dictates the entire course of the dispute. It strengthens the copyright owner's position immensely, giving them massive leverage from the very first day and often forcing the infringer to seek a quick settlement rather than fight an uphill battle they are legally presumed to lose.

5.4: Global Perspectives: The Role of Registration Outside the U.S.

The American system, with its strong emphasis on registration as a key to unlocking remedies and powerful evidence, is actually the exception, not the rule. It's a unique model, and it's critical for anyone operating internationally to understand that the U.S. approach is not universal. Most of the world operates on a completely different philosophy, one rooted in the Berne Convention.

The Berne Convention: The "No Formalities" Rule

The foundational treaty for global copyright is the Berne Convention for the Protection of Literary and Artistic Works. A core principle, found in Article 5(2), is that copyright protection must be automatic. It explicitly states that the "enjoyment and exercise" of these rights "shall not be subject to any formality."

What does this mean? It means that in the 180+ countries that have signed this treaty (including the U.S.), an author is granted full copyright protection the instant they create a work and "fix" it in a tangible medium (like writing it down, recording it, or saving the file). You don't have to register it. You don't have to put a © notice on it. You don't have to do anything. You create it, you own it. Period.

The U.S. system, which requires registration as a prerequisite for U.S. authors to even file a lawsuit for infringement, is in direct tension with this "no formalities" rule. Most other countries adhere to the Berne standard far more strictly.

Pure Automatic Systems: The UK and Droit d'Auteur

Many countries follow the Berne model completely. In the United Kingdom, for example, there is no government-run, official registry for copyright in works like books, songs, or paintings. It simply doesn't exist. Protection is 100% automatic upon creation. When a dispute arises, ownership is proven in court just like any other fact—with evidence like dated files, contracts, drafts, and testimony.

This philosophy is even stronger in civil law countries like Germany and France, which operate on the droit d'auteur (or "author's rights") tradition. In this view, a creative work is not just a piece of property; it's a profound extension of the author's personality and intellect. These "moral rights"—like the right to be named as the author and the right to protect the work from being mutilated—are considered personal and often cannot be sold.

In this tradition, the very idea of a mandatory government registration system is nonsensical. It would be like asking someone to register their own personality. Any "deposit" systems that do exist in these countries are typically voluntary, often privately run, and serve only one purpose: to create a piece of evidence establishing a date of creation (date certaine). They are not required to have rights, and they are not required to go to court.

The "Middle Ground": Voluntary and Evidentiary Systems

Many other jurisdictions have found a middle path. They fully embrace the Berne principle of automatic protection (so registration is not required to sue) but still offer a voluntary registration system that provides powerful legal benefits, similar to the U.S. prima facie rule.

Spain is a perfect example. Its intellectual property registry is completely voluntary. You have full copyright protection without it. However, registering your work provides very strong prima facie evidence of ownership, making litigation much simpler.

Canada is similar. The Canadian Intellectual Property Office (CIPO) maintains a copyright register. Registration is not mandatory, but if you do register, your certificate serves as presumption of ownership, and the burden shifts to the defendant to prove otherwise.

The Pragmatic Approach: China

Then you have a major jurisdiction like China. On paper, China is a Berne Convention member, and its copyright law grants automatic protection. Legally, registration is voluntary.

In practice, however, the Chinese legal system places an enormous emphasis on formal, official, documentary evidence. A judge or administrative official will almost always favor the party holding an official-looking certificate with a government stamp (or "chop").

Therefore, voluntary registration with the Copyright Protection Centre of China (CPCC) is of immense practical importance. A CPCC certificate is treated as powerful prima facie proof of ownership. Without it, it is exceptionally difficult to get administrative enforcement (like customs seizures of pirated goods) or to succeed in court. So, while it is de jure (by law) voluntary, it is de facto (in reality) an essential and indispensable step for anyone serious about enforcing their rights in China.

This global tour makes one thing clear: copyright strategy cannot be "one-size-fits-all." What is a mandatory prerequisite in the United States is a helpful-but-voluntary tool in Spain, a philosophical non-starter in France, and a de facto necessity in China.

Part III: Navigating the Systems: A Comparative Guide to Registration

Navigating the Systems: Part 1 - The Americas & UK

Sub-topic 6.1: United States: The U.S. Copyright Office (USCO) Process

In the United States, the copyright system presents a fascinating blend of automatic protection and powerful, formal registration. While your copyright is technically born the moment you create and "fix" a work (like typing it on a computer), securing the full force of the law really hinges on formal registration. This process is managed by the U.S. Copyright Office (USCO), which is a part of the esteemed Library of Congress. Think of it this way: creation gives you the right, but registration hands you the shield and sword to protect it.

The most practical and cost-effective path by far is the electronic Copyright Office (eCO) system. This online portal is the central hub for creators.

First, you'll need to create an account. This is a straightforward step on the copyright.gov website. It establishes you as a user in their system, allowing you to file applications, track their status, and communicate with the office.

Next comes the most critical decision: selecting the correct application. The eCO system isn't a one-size-fits-all solution. For a straightforward literary work, like a novel written by a single author, the "Single Application" is your best bet. It's designed for simplicity and has a lower fee (currently $45). However, if your project is more complex—perhaps you co-wrote a book or the publisher is the "claimant" (the legal owner)—you must use the "Standard Application" (currently $65). There is also a very useful option for prolific creators: the "Group of Unpublished Works" (GRUW) application. This allows you to register a bundle of up to ten related unpublished works, like a collection of poems or short stories, for a single fee.

Once you've chosen your path, you must complete the application form. This is where you provide the core details of your work. You'll list the title, the full legal names of the author(s), and the name and address of the copyright claimant. The claimant is the person or entity that actually owns the copyright, which may be the author or a company they've assigned rights to. You also need to state the year the work was completed and, if it has been published, the date and nation where it was first released.

With the form filled out, you'll be directed to pay the filing fee. The eCO system links directly to the U.S. Treasury's Pay.gov portal, where you can pay securely with a credit card or a bank transfer (ACH). It's crucial to use the electronic system, as paper applications are strongly discouraged. Their filing fee is significantly higher ($125), and the processing time stretches from months into potentially over a year.

The final and most important step is submitting your deposit copy. The USCO requires a nonreturnable copy of your work for the official records of the Library of Congress. For works that only exist electronically (like an ebook or an unpublished manuscript) or were first published online, this is easy: you simply upload a digital file. However, if your work was first published in a physical format in the U.S., you must mail a physical copy of the "best edition" of that work. The "best edition" is a legal term meaning the highest quality version publicly available. For a book, this means sending the hardcover edition, not the paperback.

Only when all three elements—the completed application, the correct fee, and the deposit copy—are received by the USCO does the clock start. An examiner will review your file. If everything is in order, a certificate of registration is issued. This can take several months, but that certificate is a powerful legal tool. It serves as prima facie evidence in court, meaning a judge will accept it as proof of your ownership unless the opposing side can definitively prove otherwise.

Sub-topic 6.2: Canada: The Canadian Intellectual Property Office (CIPO) Process

Canada's approach to copyright feels refreshingly straightforward, operating on a system of trust and automation. Much like the UK, Canada fully embraces the Berne Convention, meaning copyright protection is automatic and immediate upon a work's creation. You are not required to register your work to be protected, nor do you need to register it to take an infringer to court.

So, why does the Canadian Intellectual Property Office (CIPO) even offer a voluntary registration system? The answer lies in one powerful word: evidence.

Imagine you are in a legal dispute. Without registration, the burden of proof is on you. You must prove to the court that you are, in fact, the author and owner of the work, and when you created it. This can involve digging up old files, drafts, and email records. However, if you have a CIPO certificate of registration, the legal situation flips entirely. The certificate serves as official, presumptive evidence. The court automatically presumes that you are the owner and that copyright exists in the work. The burden of proof now shifts to the other party; they must prove you aren't the owner. This is a massive strategic advantage in any legal battle, and it's the primary benefit of the modest CIPO filing fee.

The registration process itself is designed to be simple and can be completed entirely online. First, you must create a general Government of Canada account (often a "GCKey") to access CIPO's online services. This isn't a special CIPO-only account but your general key to federal government portals.

Once logged in, you file an application. The online form is direct and asks for the essential information: the title of your work, the category it falls into (such as "literary work," "artistic work," or "dramatic work"), and the full name and mailing address of the copyright owner or owners.

You will also be required to make a declaration. This is a simple statement where you identify your relationship to the work. You must declare that you are either the author, the copyright owner (if the rights were transferred to you), an assignee (someone who has purchased or been given the rights), or a licensee (someone who has been granted specific rights to use the work).

Finally, you pay the fee to complete the filing. This fee is payable by credit card or from a pre-funded deposit account with CIPO. Once this is paid and the application is accepted, you are registered. That's it. There are no further fees required to maintain the registration; it is valid for the entire copyright term.

Speaking of the term, it's vital to note a recent and significant change. As of December 30, 2022, Canada extended its general term of copyright protection. It used to be the life of the author plus 50 years. Now, it is the life of the author plus 70 years. This was a major development, bringing Canada in line with its key trading partners like the United States and the European Union, and providing a longer period of commercial value and protection for creators and their heirs.

Sub-topic 6.3: United Kingdom: The Absence of a Formal Register

The United Kingdom takes the Berne Convention's principle of automatic protection to its logical conclusion. Here, the system is beautifully simple, or perhaps, depending on your perspective, frustratingly abstract. There is no official government register for copyright.

Copyright in an original work springs into existence automatically, like a spark, at the very moment it is recorded in a fixed form. This could be typing words into a document, saving a digital photo, or recording a melody. From that instant, your work is fully protected by law. You do not need to file an application, pay a fee, or put a © symbol on it.

The UK Intellectual Property Office (IPO) is the main government body for IP, but its administrative duties are focused on rights that require registration: patents, trademarks, and registered designs. When it comes to copyright, the IPO's role is one of guidance and policy, not administration. It provides excellent resources on what copyright is and how to manage it, but it will not "register" your manuscript.

This lack of a central register creates a unique challenge. If protection is automatic, how do you prove in a dispute that you created a specific work on a specific date? The

UK system is built entirely on evidence. Authors and publishers who want a safety net must create their own dated proof of ownership.

Several common methods are used, with varying degrees of reliability:

Depositing with a Professional: The most traditional and robust method is to deposit a physical copy of your work with a trusted third party, such as a solicitor (lawyer) or a bank. They will store the sealed package and provide a dated receipt. This is strong evidence, as a solicitor is an officer of the court.

The "Poor Man's Copyright": A well-known but legally shaky method is to send a copy of your work to yourself by registered mail (like Special Delivery) and then keep the envelope sealed and stored safely. The idea is that the official, dated postmark serves as proof. However, most legal experts advise against relying on this. It's not foolproof, as an envelope could theoretically be steamed open and tampered with, weakening its value in court.

Commercial Registration Services: This is the modern solution that bridges the gap. Private companies (like the UK Copyright Service) offer a third-party deposit service. You upload your digital file to their secure system, and they issue a certificate of registration, logging the exact date and content of your work.

It is absolutely essential to understand what these methods are—and what they are not. They do not grant, create, or enhance your copyright in any way. Your copyright already exists in its full capacity. These methods are purely evidentiary. They are tools for creating a reliable, dated, third-party record that you can produce in court to prove your claim of authorship.

Sub-topic 6.4: Brazil: Registration with the National Library Foundation (FBN)

Brazil's system, like other Berne Convention signatories, grants automatic copyright protection the moment a work is created. You do not have to register your work for it to be protected. However, the Brazilian legal culture places an immense value on formal, official documentation. As a result, voluntary registration is highly encouraged and is a standard practice for serious creators and publishers.

Having an official certificate of registration is considered an invaluable asset in the event of infringement. In the Brazilian legal system, it provides a powerful, state-backed presumption of ownership that is difficult for an opponent to challenge.

For literary works, the primary and most traditional registration body is the National Library Foundation (Fundação Biblioteca Nacional - FBN), which operates under the authority of the Ministry of Culture. This is the government's official method. In the past, this process was known for being cumbersome and paper-based, but as of late 2022, the FBN has significantly modernized its system. Applicants can now file online through the central GOV.BR platform, which streamlines access for all creators.

The registration procedure, however, remains formal and detailed:

Submit an Application: You must complete the official application form, providing the key details about the work (suchA as title and genre) and the author(s).

Provide Required Documentation: This step shows the system's thoroughness. An individual applicant typically needs to provide two copies of the work (even for online applications, this deposit is key), a copy of their taxpayer ID (CPF) and personal ID (RG), and proof of residence. If a representative is filing, a power of attorney is also needed.

Pay Official Fees: A government processing fee (Guia de Recolhimento da União - GRU) must be paid to move the application forward.

Examination and Issuance: This is not a simple rubber-stamp process. The FBN conducts a formal analysis of the application and the deposited work. This thoroughness, combined with a backlog, means the process is not quick. It currently takes approximately 12 months, and sometimes longer, to receive the final certificate of registration.

For those who find the FBN's timeline too slow, an innovative alternative has emerged. The Brazilian Book Chamber (Câmara Brasileira do Livro - CBL), a respected industry body, offers its own registration services. Most notably, this includes cutting-edge methods like blockchain-based registration. This service allows a creator to certify the authorship and ownership of their work by creating a "hash" (a unique digital fingerprint) of the file and logging it on a public, immutable blockchain. This creates an immediate, tamper-proof, and globally verifiable timestamp, offering a much faster, high-tech method for establishing a date of creation.

Navigating the Systems: Part 2 - Europe & Australia

Sub-topic 7.1: Germany: The "UrhG" and the Limited Role of the DPMA

In the landscape of intellectual property, Germany stands as a cornerstone of the continental European droit d'auteur, or "author's right," system. This tradition is fundamentally different from the common law "copyright" system seen in places like the United States or the United Kingdom. The German approach is codified in its primary copyright law, the Urheberrechtsgesetz (UrhG), which translates to the "Author's Rights Act."

The very first principle of the UrhG is that protection is immediate and automatic. The moment a creator brings an original work into existence—be it a novel, a piece of music, a photograph, or a piece of software—it is protected. There are no forms to fill out. There is no fee to pay. There is no government office to notify. The right simply is, born at the same instant as the creation. This automatic protection makes Germany, like most of the world, compliant with the Berne Convention, which does away with the need for such "formalities."

What truly defines the German system is its philosophical core. The UrhG views a creative work as an extension of the author's own personality. This creates a powerful, intrinsic link that cannot be severed. Because of this, the law makes a critical distinction between two types of rights.

First are the Urheberpersönlichkeitsrechte, or the "moral rights" of the author. These include the right to be identified as the creator (right of attribution), the right to decide when and how the work is first published, and the right to protect the work's integrity from distortion or damage that would harm the author's reputation. These moral rights are considered so personal that they are inalienable. An author cannot sell or transfer them, ever. They remain with the author until death and are then protected by their heirs.

Second are the Verwertungsrechte, or the "exploitation rights." These are the economic rights: the right to copy, distribute, display, and adapt the work. These are what we typically think of as copyright. In Germany, even these cannot be "sold" in their entirety, as in a complete transfer of ownership. Instead, an author grants specific licenses (Nutzungsrechte) to publishers, producers, or others, allowing them to use the work in specific ways for a specific time. The underlying right, however, always remains with the creator.

This leads to a common point of confusion: where does one "register" a copyright in Germany? The simple answer is that you don't. There is no general government registry for this purpose. The Deutsches Patent- und Markenamt (DPMA), which is the German Patent and Trade Mark Office, is a powerhouse for "industrial" property. It expertly handles patent applications, trademark registrations, and industrial designs. But if you send them your novel or your song, they will have no mechanism to register it.

The DPMA has exactly one, very narrow, and highly specific function in the copyright world. This function relates only to anonymous and pseudonymous works. Normally, copyright in Germany lasts for the author's entire life plus 70 years. But if a work is published anonymously, the law can't use the author's death as a benchmark. So, a different rule applies: the copyright expires 70 years after the work was first published.

The DPMA maintains a special register (under § 138 of the UrhG) to address this. An author who published under a pseudonym, or their heirs after their death, can file an entry in this register to state their real name. If they do this, the clock switches. The term of protection reverts from "70 years after publication" back to the standard, and usually much longer, "70 years after the author's death." This is a highly specialized tool for managing the copyright term, not a system for establishing authorship or ownership in the first place. For the vast majority of creators in Germany, proof of authorship relies on keeping good records: dated drafts, email correspondence, and other evidence that establishes a timeline of creation.

Sub-topic 7.2: France: Automatic Protection and Evidentiary Deposits

France is, in many ways, the historical and philosophical heartland of the droit d'auteur system. The French concept of an "œuvre de l'esprit," or a "work of the mind," is central to its legal tradition. This concept is broad and elegant, covering any creation that is original, meaning it bears the imprint of the author's personality. As soon as such a work is created, the Code de la propriété intellectuelle (French Intellectual Property Code) automatically grants it full and robust protection.

Similar to Germany, this protection is absolute and requires no formal steps. The rights exist from the moment of creation, not the moment of registration. There is no mandatory or official government copyright office. The Institut National de la Propriété Industrielle (INPI), or the National Institute of Industrial Property, is the French public body in charge of industrial property—patents, trademarks, and industrial designs. It does not handle copyright registration.

This automatic system creates a practical challenge. If copyright is automatic, and two people claim to have written the same song, how does a court decide who is telling the truth? The legal right may be automatic, but the proof of that right is not.

To solve this problem, France has a well-established culture of using voluntary deposit systems. It is critical to understand that these systems do not grant, create, or enhance copyright. The copyright already exists. These deposits are purely evidentiary. They are tools designed to create a prima facie (at first glance) piece of evidence that a specific work existed in a specific form on a specific date, linking it to a specific person. In a legal dispute, this can be incredibly valuable.

Authors in France have several options for creating this certified date of creation:

The INPI's "e-Soleau" Envelope: This is a modern, accessible, and official service offered by the very agency that doesn't register copyright. The e-Soleau envelope is a purely digital, low-cost solution. A creator can upload their files (a manuscript, source code, a design, a musical composition) to the INPI's secure system. The INPI then digitally time-stamps the deposit and holds it for a period of five years, which can be renewed. This provides an undisputed, government-certified "certain date" of creation.

Collective Management Organizations (CMOs): These are perhaps the most traditional and respected routes. Various organizations representing different types of creators offer deposit services for their members. For example, the Société des Auteurs et Compositeurs Dramatiques (SACD) serves playwrights and screenwriters. Depositing a script with the SACD provides a powerful piece of evidence within that specific industry. Other bodies, like the Société des Gens de Lettres (SGDL) for literary authors, offer similar services.

Private Services: A market of private companies and notaries (huissiers de justice) also offers to hold copies of works and provide a certified date. These function on the same principle, acting as a trusted third-party witness to the work's existence at a point in time.

In the French system, the creator is born with the right. The focus is not on registering that right, but on prudently preparing for the day you may have to defend it. These evidentiary deposits are not a legal shield, but rather a sharpened sword, ready to be used if a dispute ever arises. They are a practical, common-sense solution to a problem created by a system of powerful, invisible, and automatic rights.

Sub-topic 7.3: Spain: Voluntary Registration with the Intellectual Property Register (RPI)

Spain's copyright system presents a fascinating and highly practical hybrid model. It fully aligns with the European Union and the Berne Convention, meaning that, just like in Germany and France, copyright protection is automatic. An author's rights spring into existence the very moment a creative work is completed. There is absolutely no requirement to register the work to gain this protection. You can write a novel, publish it, and sue for infringement without ever having filed a single piece of paperwork with the government.

However, Spain diverges from its neighbors by offering something they do not: a formal, centralized, and government-run voluntary registration system. This is the

Registro de la Propiedad Intelectual (RPI), or the General Intellectual Property Register, which is managed by the Ministry of Culture.

So, the immediate question is: if protection is already automatic, why would anyone bother to go through the process and pay the fee to register their work?

The answer lies in a powerful legal concept: the "presumption of authorship." This is the single most important benefit of the RPI and the reason it is so highly recommended by legal professionals in Spain. Let's unpack what this means in practice.

If you do not register your work and someone infringes it, you must take them to court. In court, the burden of proof is on you. You must first prove to the judge that you are, in fact, the author and that you created the work on a certain date. You would have to produce drafts, emails, and other evidence.

If you do register your work with the RPI, the situation is completely reversed. You walk into court and present your official RPI certificate. This registration creates a strong iuris tantum legal presumption—meaning it is presumed to be true unless proven otherwise. The judge now assumes you are the author and owner of the rights listed in the register. The burden of proof is no longer on you; it shifts entirely to the person you are accusing. They must now prove that the official government register is wrong and that you are not the author. This is a massive strategic advantage in any legal dispute, effectively making the registration a powerful shield.

The registration process itself is formal but straightforward. An application can be filed at any of the RPI's provincial offices or, increasingly, online. The applicant must submit a copy of the work (e.g., a physical book, a digital file), details about the author or authors, information about who holds the rights (if different from the author), and pay a small administrative fee.

The RPI's staff will then check the application to ensure all formal requirements are met—that the forms are correct and the work is eligible for protection. They do not judge the work's quality or originality; they simply administer the register. Once approved, the work is entered into the central database, and the applicant receives a certificate that provides this powerful legal presumption. For authors, publishers, and producers in Spain, this system is seen as a crucial, low-cost insurance policy that formalizes their claims and dramatically strengthens their position from the very beginning.

Sub-topic 7.4: Australia: Automatic Protection and the Absence of a Register

When we navigate to Australia, we leave the European droit d'auteur tradition and enter a system based on British common law. The Australian approach, governed by the Copyright Act 1968, is philosophically different but arrives at a similar starting point: copyright protection is free, automatic, and requires no registration.

The key trigger for protection in Australia is the moment an original literary, dramatic, musical, or artistic work is "recorded in a material form." This is a crucial distinction. An idea for a novel or a melody in your head is not protected by copyright. But the instant you record that idea—by writing it down, typing it into a computer, sketching it on paper, or capturing it in an audio file—it is protected. "Material form" is interpreted very broadly to include any method of storage from which the work can be reproduced.

The most defining feature of the Australian system is its complete absence of an official government copyright register. This often surprises people familiar with the U.S. Copyright Office.

The government agency IP Australia is the central body for intellectual property, but its role is strictly defined. It is responsible for registered rights: patents for new inventions, trademarks for brand names and logos, and registered designs for the visual appearance of a product. Copyright, as an unregistered right, falls completely outside its jurisdiction. IP Australia does not administer, register, or maintain any records of copyright ownership.

This "no register" system places the entire burden of proof squarely on the shoulders of the creator. If your copyright is infringed, it is 100% your responsibility to prove two key things in court:

That you are the original author.

That you created the work at a specific time (before the infringer did).

Since there is no official certificate to rely on, Australian creators must be diligent about evidence management. Best practices are not just suggestions; they are essential components of enforcing your rights.

First is the use of the copyright notice, such as © 2025 Author's Name. In Australia, this notice is not legally required to secure protection (as a Berne Convention member, protection is automatic). However, its practical and legal value is immense. It acts as a clear warning to the public that you are claiming rights. More importantly, it prevents an infringer from using the "innocent infringement" defense in court. An infringer who copies a work clearly marked with a notice cannot claim they didn't know it was protected, which generally allows the rights holder to claim a wider range of damages.

Second, and most importantly, is keeping meticulous records. This is the Australian equivalent of a registration certificate. Creators must keep dated drafts, digital files with their original metadata, email correspondence with editors or publishers, and any other evidence that establishes a clear timeline of the creative process.

A common myth is the "poor man's copyright"—the idea of mailing a copy of your work to yourself in a sealed, postmarked envelope. This is an unreliable and outdated practice. A court may give it little weight, as envelopes can be tampered with. Far more robust evidence comes from digitally verifiable sources or simply a well-organized archive of your creative journey. In Australia, the system grants the right for free, but it trusts you, the creator, to be the archivist and defender of your own work.

Navigating the Systems: Part 3 - Asia & Other Key Jurisdictions

Sub-topic 8.1: China: The Strategic Importance of Voluntary Registration with the CPCC

The intellectual property landscape in China operates on a fascinating dual system. On one hand, China is a signatory to the Berne Convention. This means, legally, that copyright protection is automatic. The moment an author, artist, or programmer completes an original work, it is theoretically protected by law. No forms, no fees, no applications are required to have the copyright. This is the law.

However, there is also the practical reality. This is the world of courtrooms, administrative enforcement, and e-commerce platforms. In this world, proving you are the one who created that work—especially if you are a foreign entity—is a massive challenge. This is where the Copyright Protection Centre of China (CPCC) becomes one of the most powerful strategic tools in a creator's toolkit.

Voluntary registration with the CPCC, an official body operating under the National Copyright Administration (NCA), is not about creating your right. It's about proving it. The registration certificate issued by the CPCC acts as prima facie proof of ownership. This simple-sounding legal term is the key to everything. It means that, in the eyes of the law, the certificate is accepted as true "on its face." The burden of proof shifts. With that certificate, you are presumed to be the owner. Without it, the burden is entirely on you to prove you are.

The "Golden Ticket" in Court

Chinese courts and administrative bodies have a strong, culturally ingrained preference for formal, government-issued documentary evidence. A judge or official is far more comfortable, and will act far more quickly, when presented with an official, stamped certificate from a Chinese government body than with a stack of your internal "proof."

Imagine this scenario: A company in another country finds its software, which it spent two years developing, being sold on a Chinese website.

Scenario A (Without a CPCC Certificate): The company must sue. To prove it owns the software, it must gather its internal development logs, emails between programmers, source code drafts, and employee contracts. Because all this evidence is from a foreign country, it must all be notarized in the home country. Then, it must be taken to the Chinese embassy or consulate in that country for legalization. This entire package must then be translated into perfect, legally-sound Mandarin. This process can take months and cost thousands of dollars, all before the case even begins. All this time, the infringer continues to sell the software.

Scenario B (With a CPCC Certificate): The company's lawyer walks into court and presents the CPCC registration certificate. The judge sees the official stamp. The burden of proof immediately shifts to the infringer. The infringer must now prove that the certificate is wrong or fraudulent. This is an incredibly difficult, and often impossible, position for them. The case can be expedited, and an injunction to stop the sales can be issued much, much faster.

This certificate effectively acts as a golden ticket, allowing you to bypass the long, expensive, and uncertain process of validating foreign evidence.

The Battlefield of E-Commerce Takedowns

The most common form of infringement today happens online. Platforms like Alibaba, Tmall, Taobao, and JD.com handle millions of listings. They do not have time to conduct lengthy investigations into who really created a product. They rely on simple, clear-cut "notice-and-takedown" procedures.

To fight infringement on these platforms, you must first register an account on their own intellectual property (IP) protection portal, such as Alibaba's "IPR" platform. To do this, you must upload proof of your IP rights.

This is where the CPCC certificate shines. It is the single most effective, most recognized, and most rapidly accepted form of proof for these platforms. When you file a complaint against an infringing listing and attach your CPCC certificate number, the platform's internal team can verify it quickly. In many cases, the infringing listing is taken down within days or even hours.

Without it, you are back to Scenario A. You would have to submit your notarized, legalized, and translated home-country evidence. The e-commerce platform's review team is likely to see this complex bundle of foreign documents as confusing and slow. They may deny the request, asking for "clearer proof"—which is exactly what the CPCC certificate provides.

The Simple, Inexpensive Process

Given its immense value, you might expect the registration process to be difficult. It is not. It is relatively straightforward and inexpensive.

Application: An application is filed online, which includes details about the author, the owner, and the work itself.

Submission: You must submit a sample of the work. For a book, this might be a manuscript. For a graphic, the image. For software, which is a critical and very common type of registration, this typically means submitting the first and last 30 pages of the source code and a user manual.

Language: All documents must be submitted in Chinese. This is why most foreign applicants use a local Chinese agent or law firm to handle the filing.

Cost: The official government fees are modest, often ranging from 100 to 2,000 RMB depending on the work. For software registration, the official fee was actually abolished, making it free (though you still pay your agent).

Timeline: The entire process, from filing to receiving the certificate, typically takes between one and three months.

When you compare a few hundred dollars and a two-month wait to a multi-thousand-dollar, six-month-plus legal nightmare, the strategic value is undeniable. It is a small, one-time investment that provides foundational security for any creative work intended for the Chinese market. It is, quite simply, an essential cost of doing business.

Sub-topic 8.2: Japan: Automatic Protection and the Role of the JCO

Japan's copyright system presents a clear and powerful contrast to the practical situation in China. Japan is not only a member of the Berne Convention, but its legal system fully embraces the convention's core principle: copyright protection is absolute and automatic from the moment of creation.

When a work is created, it is protected. There are no forms to file. There are no fees to pay. There is no registration required to claim ownership or to enforce your rights in court. Your copyright simply exists.

Furthermore, Japanese law makes a very important and strong distinction between two types of rights, which is key to understanding its system:

Economic Rights: These are the rights you can sell, license, or transfer. This is the "bundle of rights" that includes the right to reproduce, to broadcast, to perform, to translate, and to distribute the work. These are a form of property.

Moral Rights: These rights are not property. They are considered an extension of the author's personality and are non-transferable. They always remain with the original creator, even if the creator sells the economic rights. These include the right to be named as the author (authorship), the right to decide when and how the work is first published (divulgence), and the right to prevent the work from being changed or distorted in a way that harms the author's honor (integrity).

This automatic system is robust. So, why does Japan even have a registration system? The answer is that the Japan

Copyright Office (JCO), which is part of the Agency for Cultural Affairs, does not register copyright. It registers facts. It acts as a public ledger, or a "registry of deeds," to record specific pieces of information for legal and evidentiary certainty.

Registering Facts, Not Creation

The JCO's registration system is not used to prove you created a work. It's used to prove specific transactional or factual details about that work, which can be very important in disputes. The most common registrations are:

Registration of True Name: If you publish a book under a pseudonym (a pen name) or anonymously, you can later register your true name with the JCO. The legal effect is powerful: you are now presumed to be the author. This also has a major impact on the copyright term, which for an anonymous work is 70 years from publication, but for a named author is 70 years from their death.

Registration of the Date of First Publication: You can register the date your work was first published or made public. The legal effect is that your work is presumed to have been published on that date. This is critical for establishing the 70-year copyright term for anonymous or pseudonymous works.

Registration of the Date of Creation (for Software): A special rule exists for computer programs, allowing the author to register the date the software was created. This can be valuable evidence in a dispute.

The Most Important Registration: The Transfer of Rights

The single most important function of the JCO's registration system involves the transfer of economic rights. This is the "transactional tool" mentioned in the prompt, and it solves a specific legal problem often called "dual assignment" or the "third-party problem."

Let's use an analogy. Imagine you own a house. You sell that house to Person A and give them a signed contract. You have legally sold the house. But if Person A doesn't go to the city's land registry office to record the new deed, a problem can arise.

What if you, the original (and now fraudulent) owner, turn around and sell the same house to Person B? Person B, who knows nothing about Person A, gives you the money, and you sign a contract with them.

Now there are two people who "own" the house. Who wins? In many legal systems, the person who records the deed first wins.

This is exactly how copyright transfer registration works in Japan.

A novelist (the author) sells the economic rights to his novel to Publisher A. The contract is signed. Publisher A now owns the rights.

But Publisher A forgets to register this transfer with the JCO.

The novelist, being dishonest, turns around and sells the same rights to Publisher B.

Publisher B, knowing nothing of the first sale, immediately registers the transfer with the JCO.

In a legal dispute between Publisher A and Publisher B, Publisher B will win.

The law states that a transfer of copyright cannot be asserted against a third party unless it is registered. The JCO registration system provides what is known as "perfection" of the right. It's not about making the sale valid between the author and Publisher A. It's about making that sale enforceable against the rest of the world.

Therefore, while registration is not required for creation, it is an absolutely essential, non-negotiable step for any company or individual who is buying, selling, or licensing copyright in Japan. It is a simple, quick (often taking about a month), and inexpensive procedural step that secures a potentially multi-million dollar investment against future claims.

Sub-topic 8.3: India: A Deep Dive into the Copyright Registration Process

In the landscape of intellectual property, India presents a fascinating and practical model. Its legal framework, rooted in the Copyright Act of 1957, fully embraces the core principle of the Berne Convention. This means that copyright protection in India is automatic. The very moment an author fixes an original work in a tangible form—whether by typing a sentence, painting a stroke, or recording a note—the copyright for that work legally exists. There is no forms to fill out and no fee to pay for this fundamental protection to be born.

However, the 1957 Act wisely acknowledges the vast difference between having a right and proving you have that right in a court of law. This is where the Indian Copyright Office, which operates under the Ministry of Education, comes into play. The Act establishes a formal, though entirely voluntary, registration system. While you don't need to register to be the copyright owner, it is almost universally considered a crucial, highly recommended strategic step for any serious creator or publisher.

The primary, and most powerful, benefit of this voluntary registration is the certificate it yields. This certificate, and the entry it represents in the official Register of Copyrights, is recognized by the Indian legal system as prima facie evidence. This is a legal term with profound practical consequences. It essentially means "at first sight." In an infringement lawsuit, the rights holder who presents this certificate to the court has a powerful advantage. The judge will, by default, accept the details on the certificate—such as the name of the author, the date of creation, and the ownership of the work—as true. The legal burden of proof then shifts. It is no longer the author's job to prove they own the work; it becomes the alleged infringer's job to prove the certificate is wrong. This can save an immense amount of time, money, and stress, making the enforcement of copyright significantly more straightforward.

The registration process itself has been modernized and is designed to be accessible. It can be completed almost entirely online through the official portal (copyright.gov.in).

Application and Form XIV: The first step is to create an account on the portal and meticulously fill out Form XIV. This form is the foundational document for the registration. It requires the applicant to provide precise details about the work, including its title, class (e.g., literary, artistic, musical), language, and the full names and addresses of the author, owner, and any publishers. Accuracy here is paramount, as this information will form the basis of the prima facie evidence.

Fee Payment: The process requires a statutory fee. For a literary work, for instance, the fee is currently set at ₹500. This relatively low cost is intentional, making the system accessible not just to large publishing houses but also to individual authors, artists, and creators.

Submission of the Work: The applicant must then submit a copy of the work to the Copyright Office. This can be done by uploading a digital file (like a PDF for a book or an MP3 for a song) directly through the portal or by mailing physical copies to the office in New Delhi. This deposit ensures the Copyright Office has a definitive copy of the work being registered.

The 30-Day Waiting Period: Once the application is filed, a mandatory 30-day waiting period is triggered. During this window, the details of the application are made public. This serves as a crucial "public objection" phase. Any third party who believes they have a valid claim or dispute regarding the work's authorship or ownership can file an objection with the Copyright Office.

Examination and Issuance: If this 30-day period passes without any objections, the application moves to an examiner's desk. This examiner reviews the application for completeness and basic compliance. If the application is found to be in order, the Registrar of Copyrights will formally enter the work's details into the Register of Copyrights. Following this, a certificate of registration is issued and sent to the applicant, completing the process. If an objection is received, the process pauses, and the Copyright Office may hold a hearing to resolve the dispute between the applicant and the objecting party before deciding whether to grant the registration.

A final, critical consideration is the No Objection Certificate (NOC). If the work was created by an employee as part of their job (a "work for hire") or under a specific contract with a publisher, the applicant (e.g., the author) may be required to submit an NOC from the employer or publisher. This document confirms that the employer or publisher has no objection to the author registering the copyright in their own name, clarifying the chain of ownership.

Sub-topic 8.4: Russia & South Korea: A Comparative Snapshot

The contrast between Russia and South Korea offers a compelling case study in how two nations, both signatories to the Berne Convention and thus both providing automatic copyright protection, can diverge significantly in their practical approach to registration and enforcement.

Russia: A Hands-Off Approach

The Russian Federation, through its Civil Code, fully adheres to the principle of automatic protection. Copyright exists upon creation, with no formal registration required for a work to be protected by law. The primary intellectual property body in the country, the Federal Service for Intellectual Property (Rospatent), has a role that is heavily weighted toward industrial property—patents and trademarks.

When it comesto copyright, Rospatent's role is extremely limited. It does not operate a general register for artistic or literary works like books, music, or films. Its copyright-related functions are specifically carved out for only computer programs and databases. This distinction is telling; it suggests a legal view that treats software and databases as functional, commercial assets more akin to inventions than to traditional works of authorship.

For the author of a novel or the composer of a song, there is simply no formal state registration system available in Russia. This lack of a central registry places the burden of proof squarely on the author's shoulders. If an infringement dispute arises, the author must be prepared to prove their authorship and date of creation through other means. The text points to several "alternative methods" that have become common practice. These are not state registrations but rather forms of private evidence-building.

Notary Deposit: An author can take a physical copy of their manuscript to a notary. The notary will then formally certify, with a stamp and signature, that on that specific date, the author presented that specific document. This does not prove authorship, but it creates a powerful, time-stamped piece of evidence establishing that the author possessed the work at a particular point in time.

Collecting Society Deposit: Authors can also deposit their work with a professional collecting society. This creates a record within an industry-recognized body, which can be useful in disputes, particularly those concerning royalties and distribution.

South Korea: A Robust, State-Endorsed System

South Korea, in sharp contrast, demonstrates a deep belief in the value of a formal registration system, even while also providing automatic protection under Berne. The country maintains a robust and highly recommended voluntary registration system administered by the Korea Copyright Commission (KCC), which operates under the Ministry of Culture, Sports, and Tourism.

The process in South Korea is noted for being straightforward and efficient, often concluding within just a few weeks. This low barrier to entry encourages widespread participation from creators. The KCC system is not just a passive repository; it is an active tool intended to strengthen the creator's position in the marketplace.

The key benefit of registering with the KCC is powerful and precise: it establishes a legal presumption of ownership and date of creation. This functions similarly to the prima facie evidence in India but is a cornerstone of enforcement strategy in the Korean market. This presumption fundamentally shifts the dynamic of a legal dispute. When a registered creator accuses someone of infringement, the court presumes the creator is the rightful owner and that their registered date of creation is correct.

This places the burden of proof directly on the alleged infringer. The defendant must now proactively prove to the court that the registered owner is not the true author or that their work was created earlier. This is a significant legal hurdle for the defendant to overcome and a powerful strategic tool for the rights holder. It makes copyright enforcement faster, more decisive, and less reliant on a complex and expensive battle of competing evidence. For anyone seeking to protect their work in the competitive Korean market, registering with the KCC is not just an option; it's a critical strategic step.

Appendix A: Analysis of Comparative Copyright Regimes

The provided table, "Comparative Analysis of Copyright Regimes in Key Jurisdictions," offers more than just a list of facts; it paints a vivid picture of the diverse philosophies and strategies shaping global intellectual property. When analyzed, this data reveals clear patterns and "families" of legal approaches, critical for any author or publisher planning an international strategy.

The "Pure Berne" Jurisdictions

A significant bloc of countries, primarily in Europe and the Commonwealth, embrace the "pure" form of automatic protection envisioned by the Berne Convention. The United Kingdom, Australia, Germany, and France all fall into this category.

These nations have no formal state registration system for general literary or artistic works. Their respective IP offices (like the UK's IPO or Germany's DPMA) focus on industrial property. In these jurisdictions, copyright is simply a fact that comes into existence with creation. Consequently, registration is never a prerequisite for litigation.

It is telling that these same countries (especially France and Germany) are world-renowned for their strong protection of moral rights—the droit moral (right of attribution and integrity). Their legal systems are deeply invested in protecting the author's personal, spiritual connection to the work, not just its economic value. Enforcement in these countries relies not on a registration certificate but on other evidence: publication contracts, dated drafts, correspondence, and the simple fact of publication.

The "Strategic Registration" Jurisdictions

The second major group consists of nations that, while adhering to Berne's automatic protection, have built powerful strategic incentives to encourage voluntary registration. This group includes the United States, China, India, South Korea, Canada, Brazil, Japan, and Spain. While all offer voluntary systems, the reasons for registering differ dramatically.

The "Litigation Powerhouses": United States & China

The United States stands alone with its "hard" incentive: for U.S.-based works, registration with the U.S. Copyright Office is a mandatory prerequisite for filing an infringement lawsuit. It is, quite literally, your ticket to the courthouse. Furthermore, timely registration (before infringement or shortly after publication) is the only way to unlock the most powerful weapons in the U.S. copyright arsenal: statutory damages and attorney's fees. Statutory damages allow a court to award a set amount of money per infringement, freeing the author from the difficult task of proving actual financial loss.

China operates on a similar, though slightly different, logic. Registration with the CPCC is not a legal prerequisite for a lawsuit, but it is described as "practically essential." This implies a legal culture that heavily favors official state-issued documents. Arriving in court without a registration certificate puts the plaintiff at a severe disadvantage. Like the U.S., China also provides for statutory damages (including punitive damages), making registration a critical step for meaningful enforcement in that market.

The "Evidentiary Advantage" Nations

This group, which includes India, South Korea, Canada, Brazil, Spain, and Japan, uses registration to streamline the legal process. The primary benefit in these countries is evidentiary. Registration creates prima facie evidence (India, Canada, Spain) or a legal presumption of ownership (South Korea). This doesn't unlock new types of damages—most of these countries limit damages to those based on proven loss—but it makes winning a case significantly faster and less expensive by settling the question of "who is the owner" from day one.

Key Differentiators Across the Board

Looking at the table horizontally reveals other critical divergences:

Copyright Term: While "Life + 70 years" is becoming a global standard (seen in the US, UK, EU, Canada, Brazil, Australia, Japan, and Russia), key outliers exist. India maintains a "Life + 60 years" term, and China provides "Life + 50 years." This difference has massive implications for an author's heirs and the long-term commercial life of a work.

Moral Rights: The table shows a clear divide. The United States offers famously "limited" moral rights, which apply primarily to visual arts under VARA and are otherwise handled by contract. In stark contrast, virtually every other jurisdiction—from the UK and Canada to France, Germany, Japan, and India—provides strong, explicit, and often non-transferable statutory moral rights for attribution and integrity.

Ultimately, the data confirms there is no such thing as a single "international copyright." Protection is a bundle of national rights, each requiring a distinct, market-specific strategy.

Part IV: The Lifecycle and Commercialization of Copyright

The Ticking Clock: Copyright Duration and the Entry into Public Domain

The Ticking Clock: Copyright Duration and the Entry into Public Domain

Think of copyright as a bargain. It's a deal struck between a creator and the public. In exchange for sharing their work with the world, society grants the creator a temporary, exclusive monopoly. They get to be the only one who can copy, distribute, adapt, or perform their work for a set period. This exclusivity is a powerful incentive. It encourages authors, musicians, filmmakers, and artists to invest the time, money, and emotional energy needed to create new things. It gives them a chance to earn a living from their efforts.

But this monopoly is, by design, temporary. The "ticking clock" is a foundational part of this bargain. This limited duration is the crucial balance. It ensures that while creators get their reward, the works they create don't remain locked away forever. They eventually become part of our shared cultural commons, a vast and rich treasure trove we call the "public domain."

This chapter is all about that clock. We'll look at how long the copyright "alarm" is set for in different parts of the world. More importantly, we'll explore the immense legal and creative significance of what happens when that alarm finally goes off. When a work enters the public domain, it is freed. It becomes a resource for everyone. Anyone can use it, adapt it, and build upon it for any purpose—commercial or artistic—without needing to ask for permission or pay a fee. It's how we get new adaptations of Shakespeare, modern orchestra performances of Beethoven, and new stories based on 19th-century novels.

Sub-topic 9.1: The International Standard: Life of the Author Plus 50 or 70 Years

The most common way to set the copyright clock is to link it directly to the creator's own lifespan. This approach, known as auter (author)-based copyright, is very "human." The logic is that the protection should last for the creator's entire life and then for a set period after they pass away. This post-death period is intended to provide for their immediate heirs, like their children or grandchildren, allowing the family to continue to benefit from the creator's legacy.

The first major step toward an international standard came with the Berne Convention for the Protection of Literary and Artistic Works. This landmark 1886 treaty set a minimum "floor" for copyright duration that all its member countries had to agree to. That minimum term was life of the author plus 50 years (often shortened to "life+50" or pma, from the Latin post mortem auctoris). This became the global baseline for decades. For a long time, if you knew when an author died, you could simply add 50 years to find out when their works would become public property.

However, over the last few decades, a significant international trend has emerged, pushing that term even longer. Today, the predominant standard in many of the world's largest markets is life of the author plus 70 years (life+70).

This shift was largely driven by two major economic blocs. First, the European Union moved to standardize its laws. In 1993, the EU issued a "Term Directive" that required all its member states to adopt a life+70 term. The goal was to create a single, harmonized market. Before this, a work might be protected in Germany (which already had life+70) but in the public domain in Denmark (which had life+50). The EU standardized up to the longest term. This means that across Germany, France, Spain, Italy, and all other EU members, copyright lasts for the author's life plus 70 years. The United Kingdom, even after leaving the EU, has maintained this same term.

The second major driver was the United States. For works created on or after January 1, 1978, the U.S. also uses the life+70 standard. This was put into law by the 1998 "Sonny Bono Copyright Term Extension Act." This law was famously—and controversially—nicknamed the "Mickey Mouse Protection Act." This is because the new, longer term extended the copyright on early corporate works, including the 1928 cartoon "Steamboat Willie" featuring Mickey Mouse, preventing it from entering the public domain for another 20 years. The U.S. push for this term was partly to "harmonize" with the new EU standard, ensuring American works received the same long protection in Europe that European works received in America.

This "life+70" standard has become a powerful global benchmark, often exported through international trade agreements.

Australia adopted the life+70 term, in large part due to its Free Trade Agreement with the United States.

Canada provides a very recent example. For generations, Canada was a "life+50" country. But as a condition of the new Canada-United States-Mexico Agreement (CUSMA), which replaced NAFTA, Canada was required to extend its copyright term. On December 30, 2022, Canada's copyright term officially changed from life+50 to life+70.

While life+70 is the dominant trend, not every country follows this exact model.

India, for example, has a term of life of the author plus 60 years.

Japan was a "life+50" country for over a century but extended its term to life+70 in 2018. This change was part of the Trans-Pacific Partnership (TPP) trade deal.

Mexico has one of the longest terms in the world: life of the author plus 100 years.

This "life plus" calculation gets a little more complex when a work isn't created by just one person. What about works of joint authorship? A joint work is one where two or more authors create something with the intention that their contributions be merged into one single, inseparable work. Think of a novel co-written by two authors, or a song where one person writes the music and another writes the lyrics.

In this case, the law doesn't start the clock when the first author dies. That wouldn't be fair to the other author or their heirs. Instead, the copyright term is typically calculated based on the life of the last surviving author. So, in the U.S. and the E.U., copyright in a jointly authored book will last for 70 years after the death of the co-author who dies last.

The final, wonderful result of this ticking clock is "Public Domain Day." Because these terms are based on the end of the year of death, all works scheduled to expire in a given year do so at the exact same moment: the stroke of midnight on January 1st. This has become an annual celebration for creatives, historians, and the public. In recent years, major works like F. Scott Fitzgerald's The Great Gatsby (in 2021) and A. A. Milne's original Winnie-the-Pooh (in 2022) have entered the public domain in the U.S., sparking a massive wave of new books, films, and creative adaptations.

Sub-topic 9.2: Alternative Terms: Works Made for Hire, Anonymous, and Pseudonymous Works

The "life of the author" model works perfectly when the author is a known human being. But what happens when that's not the case?

What if the "author" is a corporation, like a movie studio or a software company? A corporation doesn't have a "life" and doesn't "die."

What if the author is unknown? An anonymous work has no author listed at all.

What if the author uses a pen name? A pseudonymous work lists a fake name (like Mark Twain or George Orwell).

In these cases, you can't tie the copyright term to a person's lifespan. The law needs a different kind of clock. For these categories, legal systems provide an alternative, fixed-term duration. This fixed term provides certainty for the public and for businesses, starting the clock from a specific, objective date.

In the United States, these works are protected for a term of 95 years from the year of first publication or 120 years from the year of creation, whichever expires first.

Let's break that down, because those two numbers are very important.

"Creation" is the moment the work is fixed in a tangible form (e.g., a movie script is saved, a song is recorded, a painting is finished).

"Publication" is when the work is distributed to the public.

A work might be created (a film is shot in 1940) but not published (released in theaters until 1945). The law provides two backstops. The "120 years from creation" rule is the ultimate safety net, ensuring that even if a work is created and then hidden in a drawer for 80 years before being published, its copyright will eventually expire. The "95 years from publication" is the more common term. The law says to calculate both dates, and whichever one comes up first is the one that applies.

This fixed 95/120-year term applies to anonymous and pseudonymous works, but its most significant use is for works made for hire (WMFH). This is a critical legal concept. In this situation, the employer or the commissioning party is legally considered the "author" from the very beginning, and they own all copyright.

The U.S. defines a WMFH in two specific ways:

A work prepared by an employee within the scope of their employment. This is the most common case. If you are a salaried software developer at Microsoft, the code you write as part of your job is not yours. Microsoft is the "author" under the law, and the copyright lasts for 95/120 years. If you are a staff journalist for a newspaper, the articles you write for the paper are owned by the newspaper as WMFH.

A work specially ordered or commissioned. This is for freelancers and independent contractors, and it's much trickier. It's not enough to just pay someone. To be a WMFH, the arrangement must meet two conditions:

The parties must expressly agree in writing that the work will be considered a work made for hire.

The work must fall into one of nine specific categories listed in the law (such as a contribution to a collective work, part of a motion picture, a translation, an atlas, or a test).

This creates a common "freelancer trap." If a company hires a freelance photographer to take pictures for its website, and they don't sign a WMFH agreement, the default rule is that the photographer (the creator) owns the copyright. The company just gets a license to use the photos for the website. This distinction is a massive deal in creative industries.

What about anonymous and pseudonymous works? The fixed 95/120-year term applies unless the true identity of the author is revealed. If the author of a pseudonymous work (like J.K. Rowling writing as Robert Galbraith) is known, the term "reverts" to the standard life+70 rule, based on the real author's lifespan. An author can also ensure this by registering their true identity with the U.S. Copyright Office.

Other countries have similar, though not identical, rules for these situations.

In Japan, works authored by a corporation or published anonymously are protected for 70 years following publication.

Germany also uses a term of 70 years from publication for an anonymous or pseudonymous work. However, just like in the U.S., if the author's real identity is revealed or registered, the term reverts to the standard life-plus-70 calculation.

In the United Kingdom, the term for an anonymous or pseudonymous work is 70 years from the date it is first "made available to the public."

Finally, it's important to note one other major category: sound recordings. The copyright in a song (the sheet music and lyrics) is separate from the copyright in a specific recording of that song (the "master" track). Sound recordings often have their own unique and highly complex set of rules and durations, which can vary dramatically from country to country and depending on when the recording was made. For instance, in the U.S., sound recordings made before 1972 were governed by a patchwork of state laws until the "CLASSICS Act" recently moved them into the federal system, creating a whole new set of fixed expiration dates.

Part 1 (Sub-topic 9.3): The Public Domain: When Copyright Expires

The world of creativity is built on what came before. Every story, every song, and every painting is part of a long conversation. But for that conversation to happen, ideas must eventually be free for everyone to use. This is the core purpose of the "public domain."

Imagine a vast, shared library of human culture. When an author writes a book, they get a special, exclusive right to own, print, and sell that book for a limited time. This is called copyright. It's a way to ensure creators can make a living from their work. It's their private shelf in the library. But that right was never meant to be permanent. The "deal" of copyright is that after a set period, the creator's exclusive ownership expires. The book moves from their private shelf to the main, public collection.

Once a work enters the public domain, it belongs to everyone and no one. It is no longer protected by copyright. This means anyone—you, me, a major movie studio, a local high school—can use it for any purpose. You don't need to ask for permission. You don't need to pay royalties. You don't face any restrictions.

What does "use" mean? It means everything.

You can reproduce it. A publisher can print a brand new, low-cost edition of the book.

You can distribute it. A website like Project Gutenberg can offer it for free download to the entire world.

You can adapt it. You could turn a public domain novel into a movie, a graphic novel, a play, or a video game. You could even write a sequel, a prequel, or a modern retelling, like Pride and Prejudice and Zombies.

You can publicly perform it. A community theater can stage a play based on the work without paying a cent in licensing fees.

The public domain is not a dusty attic of forgotten works. It is a vital, living, and breathing cultural commons. It is the raw material for all new art. It's the foundation for education, research, and innovation. The Disney empire, for example, was built by adapting public domain fairy tales like Snow White and Cinderella. When F. Scott Fitzgerald's The Great Gatsby entered the public domain in 2021, it resulted in a flood of new editions, graphic novels, and even a Muppet-themed version. This is the public domain in action.

Each year, on January 1, a new class of works joins this cultural commons. This day is celebrated around the world as "Public Domain Day." It is a moment when our shared culture gets richer.

However, this process was stalled in the United States for twenty years. In 1998, Congress passed the Sonny Bono Copyright Term Extension Act. This law, often nicknamed the "Mickey Mouse Protection Act" because it kept early Mickey Mouse cartoons from entering the public domain, added 20 more years to existing copyright terms. The result was a cultural freeze. From 1999 to 2018, no published works entered the public domain in the U.S. A whole generation of culture was kept under lock and key, unavailable for new creators to build upon.

Thankfully, this deep freeze ended. Since January 1, 2019, the doors to the public domain have reopened, and the process has resumed.

On January 1, 2025, a truly monumental wave of creativity was unlocked. All works first published in the United States in 1929 became free for all. This includes some of the most significant works of the 20th century.

In literature: Ernest Hemingway's A Farewell to Arms, William Faulkner's The Sound and the Fury, and Virginia Woolf's seminal feminist essay A Room of One's Own all entered the public domain. The first English translation of Erich Maria Remarque's powerful anti-war novel, All Quiet on the Western Front, also joined them.

In film: The Marx Brothers' first feature film, The Cocoanuts, became available for free screening and remixing.

In music: Popular songs like "Singin' in the Rain" (the song, not the later film) and "Tiptoe Through the Tulips" became free to use in new movies, samples, and arrangements.

In art: René Magritte's iconic surrealist painting The Treachery of Images (the one that says "This is not a pipe") was published in 1929. In the U.S., its copyright term expired, allowing it to be reproduced on posters, t-shirts, and book covers.

This annual "unwrapping" of our shared culture is not just a legal formality. It is an act of cultural renewal. It allows archives and libraries to digitize and preserve fragile old books and films, ensuring they survive for future generations. It allows students and teachers to access and use foundational texts without barriers. And it gives new artists, musicians, and filmmakers a fresh palette of ideas to remix, critique, and celebrate. The public domain is, in essence, the future of creativity.

Part 2 (Sub-topic 9.4): International Discrepancies in the Public Domain

The idea of a single, global "public domain" is a powerful one. Unfortunately, it is a myth.

A critical and confusing point of international law is that copyright is territorial. This means a work's public domain status is "jurisdiction-specific." It is not determined by one single rule, but by the laws of the specific country where the work is being used. Just because a book is free to use in the United States does not mean it is free to use in France, Canada, or Japan.

This creates a complex and fragmented map of copyright, leading to major discrepancies for creators, publishers, and even online users. You must assess a work's status under the law of each country where you intend to use it.

Why the difference? It boils down to two different philosophies. The United States historically treated copyright as a commercial incentive—a limited monopoly to "promote the progress of science and useful arts." This led to fixed terms based on the publication date (like the 95-year term for works before 1978).

In contrast, the European "author's rights" or droit d'auteur tradition views a work as an extension of the author's personality. The law is designed to protect the author and their legacy. Therefore, their copyright term is almost always based on the author's date of death. The most common standard, adopted by the European Union, the United Kingdom, and many other nations, is "life of the author plus 70 years."

Let's look at the concrete example from 1929: Ernest Hemingway.

His novel, A Farewell to Arms, was published in 1929.

Hemingway died in 1961.

In the United States, the law for a 1929 work is a fixed 95-year term from publication.

Calculation: 1929 + 95 years = 2024.

Status: The book entered the public domain in the U.S. on January 1, 2025. A U.S. publisher can now print it freely. A U.S. filmmaker can adapt it.

In the United Kingdom (or anywhere in the EU), the law is "life plus 70 years."

Calculation: 1961 (Hemingway's death) + 70 years = 2031.

Status: The book remains under copyright until January 1, 2032. A UK publisher cannot freely issue new editions. They must still obtain a license from Hemingway's estate and pay royalties.

This one book exists in two legal states at the same time. It is free in New York, but protected in London.

This legal principle is known as lex loci delicti—the law of the place where the tort (or infringement) occurs. If a UK publisher prints the book without permission, they are breaking UK law, and the U.S. status is irrelevant.

This applies to all the works from 1929. William Faulkner's The Sound and the Fury is another perfect example.

Faulkner died in 1962.

U.S. Status: Public domain on January 1, 2025 (95 years from 1929 publication).

UK/EU Status: Copyrighted until January 1, 2033 (70 years after his 1962 death).

A filmmaker in the U.S. is free to adapt Faulkner's novel right now. A filmmaker in the UK must wait, or pay for the rights.

This puzzle gets even more complicated in the internet age. If you run a blog from Canada (which uses "life + 70") and you post a poem that is public domain in the U.S., are you infringing copyright for your readers in the UK? Where does the "use" happen? On your server in Canada? On the reader's screen in London? The law is dangerously unclear and presents a major risk for anyone sharing content online.

Even the U.S. system is a patchwork. To simplify its laws and align with the rest of the world, the U.S. finally adopted the "life + 70" standard for all works created on or after January 1, 1978.

This means that to check the status of a work in the U.S. alone, you have to ask a series of questions:

Was it published before 1929? (If so, it's in the public domain.)

Was it published between 1929 and 1977? (It's protected for 95 years from publication.)

Was it created after 1977? (It's protected for the author's life plus 70 years.)

There is no simple, single answer. The dream of a universal public domain, where all of humanity's culture is available to all people at the same time, is not our current reality. The only safe path forward is caution. Before using an older work, you must be a detective, conducting a jurisdiction-specific analysis for every country where you hope to share your new creation.

The Modern Author: Copyright Considerations for Self-Publishers and Digital Creators

10.1: The Self-Published Author as Copyright Owner and Manager

Stepping into the world of self-publishing is an incredible act of empowerment. You've shed the gatekeepers. You've decided to take your creative vision directly to the readers. This is the moment of ultimate freedom. It's also the moment you clock in for your second job: the job of publisher. This isn't just a title; it's a profound shift in responsibility. In the traditional publishing world, an author's relationship with their copyright is often one of polite distance. They create the work, and then, in a complex legal contract, they "grant" or "assign" specific rights to a publishing house. The publisher, in turn, pays an advance and royalties and takes on the heavy lifting—the editing, the marketing, the distribution, and the dense administrative work of protecting the book. The publisher registers the copyright. The publisher secures the ISBNs. The publisher drafts the legal notices.

When you self-publish, that entire support structure disappears. But in its place, you gain something far more valuable: 100% control and 100% ownership. This is the grand bargain of the modern author-entrepreneur. You keep all the keys to your kingdom. You decide the price. You decide the cover. You control the film rights, the foreign translation rights, the audiobook rights, and the merchandise rights. They are all yours, forever.

But with great power comes great, and immediate, responsibility. You are now the sole manager of your most important business asset: your intellectual property. This isn't just a "book"; it's a "property" that you must manage, protect, and leverage. This role requires a completely new mindset and a checklist of non-negotiable tasks.

First, let's talk about ISBNs. The International Standard Book Number is your book's global identifier. It's like a social security number for your product. It's how booksellers, libraries, and distributors track your book. If you're publishing on a platform like Amazon KDP, they might offer you a "free" identifier (like an ASIN). But a free identifier often lists the platform as the publisher and may not be usable on other platforms. To be a true publisher, you must acquire your own ISBNs. In the United States, these are sold exclusively by Bowker. You'll need a separate ISBN for every single format of your book. Your paperback needs one. Your hardcover needs a different one. Your ebook needs a third one. Your audiobook needs a fourth. Why? Because they are different products. A bookstore needs to know if they are ordering the $24.99 hardcover or the $15.99 paperback. The ISBN is the tracking number that makes this entire commercial system work. As the publisher, acquiring and correctly assigning these numbers is your first administrative hurdle.

Next, and most critically, is copyright registration. Here's a common misconception: your work is copyrighted the moment you create it. This is true. The moment you type "The End" on your manuscript, you own the copyright. So why bother registering it with the U.S. Copyright Office? Because registration is not about creating your right; it's about enforcing it.

Think of it this way: owning the copyright is like having the deed to a house. Registering it is like filing that deed with the county courthouse. You don't need to file it to own the house, but you absolutely need it filed if someone tries to move in and claim your house as their own.

For authors, especially those in the U.S. market, registration is a strategic weapon. If you don't register your copyright, you can't file a lawsuit for infringement in federal court. That's it. Your path to legal action is blocked. Furthermore, if you register your work before an infringement happens (or within three months of publication), you become eligible for "statutory damages" and attorney's fees. This is a game-changer. It means if someone pirates your book, you can sue for a set amount of damages (up to $150,000 for willful infringement) without having to prove you lost that specific amount of money. It also means the infringer might have to pay your lawyer's bills. This threat is often the only thing that gives a takedown notice any real power. As the self-published author, this decision—whether, when, and how to spend the small fee to register your work—rests entirely on your shoulders.

Your role as manager continues with drafting your legal notices. Every professional book has a "copyright page." In a traditional house, a legal team drafts this. As a self-publisher, you are the legal team. You are responsible for creating the copyright page, the disclaimers, and any other notices that protect you and inform the reader. This page is your legal footprint inside the book itself, declaring your ownership to the world. (We will cover exactly what goes on this page in the next section.)

Finally, there is the most challenging job: enforcement. If a traditional publisher finds a pirated copy of their author's book online, they have a legal department that swings into action. They have systems for sending DMCA (Digital Millennium Copyright Act) takedown notices. They have the resources to pursue legal action.

When you're self-published, you are the legal department. Monitoring the internet for infringement is now your direct responsibility. This means setting up Google Alerts for your book title, periodically searching pirate sites, and learning how to file a DMCA takedown notice with a website's host. It can be an exhausting, emotionally draining, and frustrating part of the job. But it is your job. Ignoring it means allowing your core business asset to be devalued.

This collection of tasks—securing identifiers, registering your asset, drafting legal notices, and enforcing your rights—is what separates a hobbyist from an author-entrepreneur. You must adopt a business-oriented mindset. Your copyright is not just a shield; it's the engine of your business. It's the asset that allows you to license your work for an audiobook, sell the translation rights to a publisher in Germany, or option the film rights to a studio. But it only has value if it is managed, maintained, and actively protected.

10.2: Crafting an Effective Copyright Page for Ebooks and Print

The copyright page is, without a doubt, the most overlooked page in a self-published book. It's typically located on the reverse side of the title page (often called the "verso"). To many new authors, it feels like a wall of boring legal text. The temptation is to find a template online, copy-paste it, and move on. This is a mistake. Your copyright page is not a formality; it's a vital piece of your book's architecture. It is your formal declaration of rights, your first line of legal defense, and a critical tool for the entire book trade. A comprehensive, professional copyright page signals to librarians, booksellers, reviewers, and readers that this is a serious work produced by a serious publisher.

Let's break down the essential elements, from the non-negotiable to the highly recommended.

First and most essential is the Copyright Notice itself. This is the core of the page. The universally recognized format is simple: © [Year of First Publication] by [Your Legal Name or Pen Name]. The "©" symbol (a "C" in a circle) is the international symbol for copyright. The "year of first publication" is the year you first made the book available to the public. And the "name" is the legal owner of the work. You can absolutely use your pen name here, as it legally connects that pseudonym to the work. For an audiobook, you will often see a "℗" symbol, which represents the copyright in the sound recording (phonogram), a separate right from the copyright in the underlying text.

Right below the notice, you must include a Rights Reserved Notice. The most common and effective phrase is simple: "All rights reserved." This three-word sentence is a powerful legal statement. It means that you, the copyright owner, reserve every single right granted to you under international copyright law. You are stating that no one can do anything with your work without your explicit permission.

Many authors go a step further with a more detailed clause, and this is highly recommended in the digital age. You've likely seen it: "No part of this book may be reproduced, distributed, or transmitted in any form or by any means, including photocopying, recording, or other electronic or mechanical methods, without the prior written permission of the publisher, except in the case of brief quotations embodied in critical reviews and certain other noncommercial uses permitted by copyright law." This language doesn't grant you new rights, but it clarifies the rules for the reader, leaving no room for ambiguity.

Next is the ISBN. As we discussed, this is your book's unique commercial identifier. You must include the correct ISBN for the specific edition the reader is holding. The paperback version will list the paperback's ISBN. The ebook version will list the ebook's ISBN. Why? This page is a primary source of information for librarians and booksellers. When a library wants to order your paperback, they will look at this page to find the exact number they need to place their order. An incorrect or missing ISBN makes your book difficult to buy, which is a critical business failure.

After the identifiers, you should include Publisher Information. As a self-publisher, you are the publisher. You have a choice here. You can simply list your own name, such as "Published by Jane Doe." However, for a much more professional appearance, you can create an "imprint." An imprint is simply a trade name for your publishing business (e.g., "Blue Sky Press" or "Main Street Books"). It creates a brand. It signals to the industry that you are operating as a business. You can list your imprint name and a contact method, such as a website or a P.O. Box. This gives booksellers and reviewers a way to contact you for bulk orders or media inquiries.

Now we move into the crucial area of Disclaimers. Disclaimers are all about limiting your liability. For works of fiction, the disclaimer is standard: "This is a work of fiction. Names, characters, places, and incidents are either the product of the author's imagination or are used fictitiously. Any resemblance to actual persons, living or dead, events, or locales is entirely coincidental." This helps protect you from potential "libel in fiction" lawsuits, where someone claims you've based a negative character on them.

For non-fiction, disclaimers are even more critical and must be tailored to your subject. If you've written a book on finance, health, or law, you must have a disclaimer. This notice clarifies that your book is providing information, not professional advice. For example: "The information in this book is for educational purposes only and is not intended as a substitute for professional medical advice. The author and publisher are not responsible for any adverse effects or consequences resulting from the use of any suggestions or procedures described in this book." This text can be your best defense if someone tries to hold you liable for their outcomes.

If your book uses borrowed material, you need a Permissions Notice. Did you include a long quote from another book? Did you use song lyrics? Did you include a photograph you didn't take? If so, you must (in most cases) get legal permission from the original rights holder. This page is where you provide the acknowledgment of that permission, such as "Excerpt from 'The Great Poem' © 2010 by John Smith, used by permission of Awesome Publishing Co." Failing to do this doesn't just look unprofessional; it's a public admission of potential copyright infringement.

Finally, a truly professional copyright page includes Credits. This is your "film credits" moment. It is professional courtesy and good business to credit the professionals who helped you. "Cover design by [Designer's Name]," "Edited by [Editor's Name]," "Interior layout by [Formatter's Name]." This does two things: It gives a valued (and often-deserved) professional nod to your team. More importantly, it signals to savvy readers that you invested in your book. You hired an editor. You hired a designer. This isn't a rough draft; it's a finished, professional product. This simple act of giving credit builds trust before the reader even gets to page one.

Sub-topic 10.3: Group Registration for Online Content: Blogs, Articles, and Social Media

The life of a modern writer has changed. Your platform isn't just a bookshelf; it's a website. Your body of work isn't just a novel; it's a thousand blog posts, a hundred online articles, and countless insightful social media threads. You are prolific. You are building an audience every single day. But this creates a serious legal problem.

Copyright protection is automatic the moment you write something. That part is free. But to enforce your copyright in court, you need to register it with the U.S. Copyright Office. If you don't register, you can't sue for infringement. More importantly, if you don't register your work before someone steals it (or within three months of its publication), you lose the right to claim statutory damages and attorney's fees. Those are the tools that give copyright law its power.

So, what is a blogger to do? Register every single 800-word post individually? At the standard application fee, registering 50 blog posts could cost you thousands of dollars. It's simply not realistic.

Recognizing this massive gap, the U.S. Copyright Office created a modern solution. It's called the Group Registration of Short Online Literary Works, or GRTX.

This option is a game-changer for digital creators. It is a single application, with a single, much lower fee, that allows you to register a group of your online works all at once. Instead of paying per piece, you pay per bundle. This tool is specifically designed for bloggers, online journalists, and any author who produces a high volume of short-form text content online.

Here is a full breakdown of how it works, what it covers, and what it doesn't.

What Qualifies for GRTX?

To bundle your work using GRTX, you must meet a specific set of rules. Every single piece in your group must qualify.

It Must Be a "Short Online Literary Work." This is the most important part. First, "literary work" means text. The GRTX registration covers only the words you wrote. It does not protect any photographs, videos, illustrations, or audio files that were in your blog post. Those require a separate registration. Second, "short" means each work must be between 50 and 17,500 words. A 40-word social media post is too short. A 20,000-word long-form essay is too long.

You Can Bundle Up to 50 Works. You can register a minimum of two and a maximum of 50 short online literary works with one GRTX application.

All Works Must Be By the Same Author. The author must be the same individual for all 50 works. The Copyright Office also allows for "joint authors," so if every post was co-written by the exact same two people, that would also qualify.

The Author Must Be the Claimant. The "claimant" is the person who owns the copyright. For GRTX, the author (or joint authors) must also be the claimant. This leads to a critical exclusion: Works made for hire are not eligible for GRTX. If you are a freelancer and you signed a contract stating your client owns the work (a "work for hire" agreement), you cannot use GRTX to register it. This option is for work you create and own yourself.

It Must Be Published Online. This option is not for unpublished drafts. Every piece in the group must have been first published on a website, a blog, a social media platform, or another online venue.

All Works Must Be Published Within a 3-Month Window. All 50 works in your application must have been published within three consecutive calendar months. For example, you could file one application for all your posts published between January 1st and March 31st. You could then file a second application for everything published between April 1st and June 30th.

The Power of GRTX: Why You Should Do It

The benefits are not just about saving money, though that is a huge factor. The standard application fee is $65. Using GRTX, you pay that same $65 fee to register up to 50 works. The savings are massive.

The real power is legal. When your GRTX application is approved, each of your 50 blog posts is treated as a separate, registered work.

Imagine a content scraper steals 20 of your registered blog posts and puts them on their own ad-filled website. Because you registered them, you can now take that scraper to court. And because each post is its own registration, you can seek separate statutory damages for each of the 20 works they infringed. This is the leverage that forces infringing websites to take your content down immediately. Without registration, your "cease and desist" letter has very little power.

How to File a GRTX Application

The process is very specific and must be followed perfectly.

Log in to the eCO System: You must file online at the U.S. Copyright Office's Electronic Copyright Office (eCO) portal. Paper applications are not accepted for this.

Choose the Right Application: Do not use the "Standard Application." You must select the option for "Register Certain Groups of Published Works" and then find "Short Online Literary Works (GRTX)."

Prepare Your Title List: You must create a list (the Copyright Office provides a fillable form) that contains the title, filename, publication date, and word count for every single work in your group.

Prepare Your Deposit Files: You must submit a copy of every work. Each work (e.g., each blog post) must be in its own separate digital file (like a .txt, .pdf, or .docx file).

Name Your Files Correctly: This is critical. The filename for each file must match the title you wrote on your title list, word for word.

Create a ZIP File: You must put all of your separate deposit files (up to 50 of them) into a single .ZIP folder. You will then upload this one .ZIP file with your application.

This process gives prolific online writers a practical, affordable, and powerful tool to protect their entire digital portfolio. It turns a chaotic collection of online content into a registered, enforceable, and valuable legal asset.

Sub-topic 10.4: Navigating Permissions: Using Third-Party Content (Quotes, Lyrics, Images)

As a self-published author, you are not just the writer. You are the CEO, the marketer, the designer, and—most importantly—the legal department. Unlike a traditional publisher, you have no dedicated "rights and permissions" team to handle legal clearances for you. That responsibility is 100% yours.

Failing to clear the rights for content you use is copyright infringement. It can get your book removed from sale, and it can lead to expensive lawsuits. Before you publish, you must secure written permission for any third-party copyrighted material you include.

This is a process that can take weeks or even months. You must plan for it long before your publication date. Here is a detailed guide to the most common types of permissions you'll need to navigate.

The Most Dangerous Trap: Song Lyrics

Writers love to use song lyrics. They evoke a mood, a time period, or a character's feelings instantly. They are also one of the most difficult and expensive things to get permission for.

There is a widespread myth that using just a few lines is "fair use." For song lyrics, this is almost always false. Because a song's lyrics are very short, a court will likely rule that even one or two lines represent a "substantial part" of the entire work. The universal advice from publishing lawyers is simple: Do not use any song lyrics without a license.

What can you do? You can use the song title and the artist's name. Titles are not protected by copyright. You can write, "He turned up the radio, and 'Like a Rolling Stone' by Bob Dylan filled the room." This is perfectly legal. You cannot write, "He turned up the radio and sang, How does it feel, to be on your own?"

If you absolutely must use the lyrics, you must:

Find the Publisher: Permission does not come from the singer. It comes from the music publisher who owns the copyright to the lyrics. You can find the publisher by searching for the song on databases run by performance rights organizations like ASCAP, BMI, or SESAC.

Request a License: You will contact the publisher's permissions department (usually via an online form). You must tell them the exact lines you want, the context of how they're used in your book, your planned print run (e.g., 5,000 copies), and all the formats you'll use (print, ebook, audiobook).

Pay the Fee: The cost is unpredictable. It could be $100. It could be thousands. One author famously reported paying £300 for just six words from one song. The fee may also need to be renegotiated if you do a second print run or a new edition.

Get a Written Contract: A verbal "OK" or an email is not enough. You must have a signed license agreement in hand before you publish.

Poetry and Book Excerpts

Poetry is treated just like song lyrics. Because poems are short, any quote beyond one or two lines is risky. An unofficial rule of thumb is that more than three lines definitely requires permission. You must contact the poet's publisher to secure a license.

Prose from other books is a bit more flexible, but you must still be careful. Using a short quote for the purpose of criticism, commentary, or review (like in a non-fiction book) may fall under fair use.

However, using a long passage, or using an excerpt in a work of fiction (for example, as an epigraph at the beginning of your chapter), is almost certainly not fair use. Some publishers have very strict internal rules, requiring permission for as few as 25 words. When in doubt, seek permission from the original book's publisher.

The Visual World: Images, Artwork, and Covers

You cannot just grab an image from a Google search. Every photograph, illustration, and piece of artwork is a copyrighted work. To use it in your book or on your cover, you must have a license.

There are three main ways to legally source an image.

Public Domain (The Best Option): These are works whose copyright has expired, or which were dedicated to the public. In the U.S., this generally includes all works published before 1926. Many museums and libraries, like the New York Public Library or the Rijksmuseum, have vast digital collections of high-resolution public domain images that you can use for free, for any purpose, with no permission needed.

Creative Commons (The "Free with Rules" Option): Creative Commons (CC) is a system where creators allow you to use their work for free, as long as you follow their specific rules. You must check the license type.

Attribution (BY): You must give proper credit. This is a non-negotiable part of almost all CC licenses. You must credit the Title, Author, Source (with a link), and License (with a link).

Non-Commercial (NC): If an image has an "NC" tag, you cannot use it for a book you are selling. This is a critical trap for self-publishers.

No-Derivatives (ND): If an image has an "ND" tag, you cannot change it. You can't crop it, add text over it, or color-filter it, making it useless for a book cover. For a book cover, you must find an image with a license that allows commercial use and derivatives, such as a CC BY or CC BY-SA license.

Stock Photo Licensing (The Standard Option): This is the most common method. You go to a site like Adobe Stock, Shutterstock, or Depositphotos and pay a fee to license an image.

You will typically purchase a "Standard License." This allows you to use the image for your book cover and modify it (add your title, author name, etc.).

Check the Limit: This is the most important part of the license. A Standard License usually has a print run limit (e.g., 250,000 or 500,000 copies). If your book becomes a bestseller and you sell more than that, you must go back and purchase an "Extended License" for a much higher fee.

Clearing permissions is a vital part of the publishing process. It is a non-negotiable legal responsibility that protects you, your book, and your career as an author.

Copyright as a Financial Asset: Valuation and Monetization Strategies

11.1 The Three Approaches to Copyright Valuation

Thinking about a copyright as a financial asset, rather than just a legal protection, opens up a new world of strategy. But before you can sell, license, or manage this asset, you have to know what it's worth. This isn't a guessing game. The art and science of "valuation" provide a formal framework for this process. Professional appraisers, who are often needed for estate taxes, sales, or litigation, don't just pull a number from a hat. They rely on three established methodologies. While one approach might take the lead, a thorough valuation will often use all three as a system of checks and balances to arrive at a defensible "fair market value."

1. The Income Approach

This is, by far, the most dominant and relevant method for valuing copyrights. Why? Because the entire point of a copyright is to produce an income stream. The Income Approach essentially asks one simple question: "How much money is this asset going to make over the rest of its life?"

To answer this, an appraiser performs a "Discounted Cash Flow" (DCF) analysis. This sounds complex, but the idea is simple.

First, they project the future net cash flows. This means estimating all the royalties from book sales, ebook sales, audiobooks, and potential licenses, year by year. Then, they subtract any expenses associated with generating that income. They must also estimate the "economic life" of the copyright. This is not just its legal term (the author's life plus 70 years). It's the commercially viable life. A hot political memoir might have an economic life of two years, while a classic children's book might have one of fifty years or more.

Second, they "discount" those future earnings back to today's value. A dollar earned ten years from now is worth less than a dollar in your pocket today, because of inflation and risk. The appraiser chooses a "discount rate," which is the "magic number" in any valuation. This rate reflects the risk of the asset. A new, unproven author's copyright is very risky; its future sales are a pure guess, so it gets a high discount rate (which lowers its present value). The copyright for a beloved author with decades of steady backlist sales is low-risk; it gets a low discount rate (which increases its present value).

The final number is the "net present value" (NPV) of the copyright. It is the single best estimate of what the asset is worth as an income-producing tool today.

2. The Market Approach

The Market Approach is much more straightforward. It's the "real estate" method. How do you value a three-bedroom house? You look at what other similar three-bedroom houses in the same neighborhood have sold for recently. This method looks for "comparable transactions," or "comps."

This approach determines a copyright's value by referencing recent sales or licensing deals for similar works. This is where it gets tricky for creative works. Every novel is, by its nature, unique. How do you find a "comp" for The Midnight Library?

However, this method becomes very powerful in specific contexts. The most famous examples are in the music industry. When Bob Dylan, Taylor Swift, or Bruce Springsteen sell their entire music publishing catalogs for hundreds of millions of dollars, those sales create public "comps." Appraisers can then analyze those deals (e.g., they sold for 20 times their average annual earnings) and apply that multiple to value another artist's catalog. In the book world, this might be used to value a portfolio of copyrights, such as the entire backlist of a genre-fiction author who has written 50 similar mystery novels.

3. The Cost Approach

This method is the least common and often the least relevant for creative works, but it's important to know. The Cost Approach values an asset based on what it would cost to re-create it.

Think about a custom software program or a technical database. You can calculate the value by adding up the costs: 1,000 hours of developer time, 200 hours of research, and so on. The value is based on the labor and materials required to build a replacement.

You can see why this fails for a novel. The material cost of writing Harry Potter was negligible (paper and ink). The "labor" cost is impossible to quantify. The value of a creative work has almost no relationship to its cost of production. Its value lies in its unique creative spark, its connection with an audience, and its market appeal. The Cost Approach simply cannot capture this. It might be used as a "floor" value for something like a textbook or a reference manual, but for most literary properties, it's a non-starter.

11.2 Factors Influencing a Copyright's Value

A copyright's value is not a fixed, static number. It is a living, breathing assessment of its financial potential, and that potential can shift dramatically based on a wide range of variables. When an appraiser (or a potential buyer) is building their valuation model, they are looking closely at these key factors. Each one can dial the final value up or down.

Historical and Projected Earnings This is the single most important factor. Past performance is the best (though not the only) predictor of future success. A copyright that has a proven, 10-year track record of generating $50,000 a year in royalties is a stable, valuable asset. A debut novel, on the other hand, is a speculative asset; it has no history, only projections. Buyers and investors will always look at the "receipts" first. A strong, consistent backlist sales history is the gold standard for high value.

Author's Status and Lifespan For a living author, their brand is intrinsically tied to the value of their entire catalog. When that author releases a new bestseller, it acts as a commercial for all their previous books. This "catalog lift" is a major financial event. An author who actively tours, maintains a large social media presence, or lands a spot in a major book club can reinvigorate their backlist and send its value soaring.

The author's lifespan is a more grim but financially critical factor. In the United States and many other territories, the copyright term is the author's life plus 70 years. This means the age of the author directly impacts the duration of the income stream. All else being equal, a copyright from a 30-year-old author has a longer potential income-producing life (their unknown lifespan + 70 years) than one from a 90-year-old author (their shorter remaining lifespan + 70 years).

Remaining Copyright Term This flows directly from the author's lifespan. Once an author passes away, the 70-year clock starts ticking. A copyright with 65 years left on its term is an asset with a 65-year income stream. A copyright with only 5 years left is a "short-term" asset, and its value will be significantly lower. The moment a work enters the public domain (like The Great Gatsby did in 2021), the exclusive right to monetize it vanishes. Anyone can publish it, and the copyright's value as a private financial asset drops to zero.

Strength and Breadth of Rights A copyright is not one single thing; it is a "bundle of rights." Imagine it's a car. Is the seller offering you the "fully loaded" model or the "base model"? A copyright where the author has retained all subsidiary rights (film, translation, audio, etc.) is the fully loaded model. It is incredibly valuable because it has numerous, unexploited income streams ready to be sold. A copyright where the author already sold off the film and translation rights to a publisher in an "all rights" contract is the base model; its potential for future monetization is much lower because those assets are already gone.

Potential for Adaptation This is the "lottery ticket" factor. A work with a high-concept plot, a unique "world," and compelling characters (think Dune, The Hunger Games, or Bridgerton) has massive "Intellectual Property" (IP) potential. The possibility of a film or television deal can add enormous speculative value to a copyright, long before any deal is ever signed. This potential is a key driver in valuation for fiction.

Market Trends and Genre No book exists in a vacuum. The specific genre and current market trends heavily influence a work's future. A vampire-themed novel was worth vastly more in the Twilight era than it was a decade prior. A cozy mystery might have a lower sales peak, but a much longer and more stable "tail" of sales, making it a reliable, long-term asset. A political tell-all might have a massive, immediate spike in value that plummets to near-zero after one or two years. The genre helps define the shape of the future income curve.

11.3 Monetization Beyond the Book: Subsidiary Rights

A common misconception is that a book's financial life begins and ends with its sale by a publisher. This is just the first step. The true, long-term wealth of a copyright is often found in what the industry calls "subsidiary rights" (or "sub-rights"). The core strategy is to unbundle the copyright.

Think of your copyright as a whole pizza. You could sell the entire pizza to one person (the publisher) in an "all rights" deal for a single price. But you would almost certainly be losing money. A savvy author or agent, however, never sells the whole pizza. They act as a "pizzeria," selling the right to different slices to different buyers, each for its own price. This strategy maximizes the total value. A good publishing contract will explicitly state which rights the publisher is licensing and which the author retains.

Here are some of the key slices that can be sold separately:

Format Rights This goes beyond just hardcover and paperback. Today, this is one of the most important categories. An author might license the print rights (hardcover and paperback) to a traditional publisher but retain the audiobook rights to license them directly to a company like Audible or to produce independently. They might also retain ebook rights. Each format is a separate market and a separate income stream.

Translation Rights This is not one right; it is dozens. It is the right to translate, produce, and sell the book in a specific language in a specific territory. An author's agent might sell German language rights to a German publisher, Japanese language rights to a Tokyo-based publisher, and Spanish language rights to a publisher in Madrid. Each of these deals comes with its own advance (an upfront payment) and its own royalty stream. Major international events like the Frankfurt Book Fair are built entirely around the buying and selling of these rights.

Serial Rights These are the rights to publish an excerpt of the book in a periodical like a magazine or newspaper. They are split into two types:

First Serial Rights: This is a high-value "teaser" that runs before the book is released. A magazine like The New Yorker might pay a significant fee for the exclusive right to print a chapter, which builds major pre-release buzz.

Second Serial Rights: This is the right to publish an excerpt after the book is already out. It's less expensive and functions more as ongoing marketing.

Book Club Rights This is the right to produce a special edition of the book specifically for a book club, like Book of the Month. These clubs buy the rights for a set fee or a royalty, print their own (often slightly different) editions, and distribute them to their large subscriber bases.

Adaptation Rights (The "Big Prize") This is the right to adapt the work into another medium. This includes film, television, stage, and even video games. This is often where life-changing money is made. Typically, a film studio won't buy the rights outright. Instead, they will "option" the rights. They pay the author a smaller fee (e.g., $10,000 - $50,000) for the exclusive right to try and develop the project for a limited time (e.g., 18 months). If the project gets a "green light" for production, the studio then "purchases" the right for a much larger, pre-negotiated sum. This creates multiple paydays for the author.

Merchandising Rights For certain genres—especially fantasy, sci-fi, and children's literature—this is a massive, long-term asset. This is the right to create and sell products based on the book's world or characters. Think of Harry Potter wands, Game of Thrones t-shirts, or Paddington Bear stuffed animals. This right is often retained by the author and can generate income for decades, long after the book sales themselves have peaked.

11.4 The Role of Collective Management Organizations (CMOs)

While an author's agent can negotiate "primary" deals for film rights or foreign translations, there is a vast category of secondary uses that are impossible for any single person to track, license, and monetize. This is the world of "micro-uses."

Think about it: an author in New York has no way of knowing that a university in Sydney, Australia, just photocopied 30 pages of their book for a course pack. They can't know that a corporation in London scanned a chapter for an internal training manual, or that a library in rural Canada just lent out their book for the 50th time. These individual uses are too small and too scattered to manage.

This is the problem that Collective Management Organizations (CMOs), or collecting societies, were created to solve.

CMOs are organizations that license works, collect royalties, and distribute that income to their members (the authors and publishers) on a collective basis. They are essentially a "union" for royalty collection. By joining a CMO, an author gives that organization the right to collect specific, hard-to-track royalties on their behalf.

Here is how the system generally works:

Licensing: The CMO issues "blanket licenses" to large-scale users. For example, a university system will pay a single annual fee to a CMO. In exchange, that fee gives the university the legal right to photocopy and scan all works in the CMO's entire repertoire for educational purposes. This is far more efficient than the university having to contact thousands of individual authors.

Tracking & Collection: The CMO collects these massive license fees from universities, corporations, government agencies, and libraries. To figure out how to divide this pool of money, they use statistical sampling. They might require the university to log all of its copying for one "survey week," or they might analyze digital records. It's an imperfect, data-driven model, but it's the only one that works at this scale.

Distribution: After taking a small administrative fee to cover its operating costs, the CMO distributes the rest of the money to its author and publisher members based on the data they collected.

For authors, CMOs are crucial for monetizing two key areas:

Photocopying and Digital Scanning: This is formally known as "reprographic" and "digital" rights. This covers course packs, corporate intranet postings, and other non-commercial re-uses of a work.

Public Lending Right (PLR): This is a specific and powerful system, particularly strong in countries like the United Kingdom, Canada, and Australia. It is not a fee paid by the library. Instead, it is a government-funded program that compensates authors for the "public service" of having their books available for free in public libraries. The CMOs in those countries (like the UK's Authors' Licensing and Collecting Society - ALCS) are often tasked by the government to track library loan data and pay authors a small fee (e.g., a few pence) for every loan.

Prominent examples like the ALCS in the UK, Access Copyright in Canada, and the Copyright Clearance Center (CCC) in the United States manage billions of these micro-transactions, turning what would otherwise be lost, unmonetizable uses into a reliable, passive income stream for authors.

The Art of the Deal: Selling, Assigning, and Licensing Your Copyright

Copyright is an asset. Like any other piece of property, it is meant to be valued, managed, and, when the time is right, exploited. For an author, this exploitation is the entire basis of their career. It is the mechanism that turns a creative spark into a commercial product and a sustainable living. The legal instruments for this exploitation are contracts. These agreements transfer or permit the use of the specific rights an author holds in their creative work.

Understanding the nuances of these agreements is perhaps the most critical business skill for any author, artist, or creator. It is, unfortunately, a skill that is often overlooked in the creative process. A brilliant manuscript can be hobbled by a bad contract, leading to decades of lost income and creative frustration. This chapter provides a practical guide to the key legal concepts and contractual terms involved in the commercialization of a literary work. We will focus on the most crucial differences between permanently selling your copyright and temporarily licensing its use, providing the foundational knowledge you need to protect your work and your future.

Sub-topic 12.1: Assignment vs. License: The Critical Distinction

The two primary mechanisms for transferring copyright interests are the assignment and the license. The distinction between them is fundamental, and it has profound, long-term consequences for an author's control over their work, their income, and their legacy.

To understand this, you must first grasp the "bundle of rights" concept. A copyright is not one single, monolithic right. It is a "bundle" of several distinct and divisible rights that the law grants to a creator. These include:

The right to reproduce the work (e.g., print copies of a book).

The right to prepare derivative works (e.g., create a movie, an audiobook, or a translation).

The right to distribute copies of the work (e.g., sell the book in stores).

The right to perform the work publicly (e.g., a play).

The right to display the work publicly (e.g., a piece of art).

Now, let's see how assignments and licenses interact with this bundle.

An Assignment: The Sale of Your Property

An assignment is a permanent transfer of ownership of the copyright itself or, more commonly, one of those exclusive rights from your bundle. It is the legal equivalent of selling a piece of real estate. When you sell your house, you sign a deed, you hand over the keys, and it is no longer yours. The new owner can live in it, rent it out, paint it, or even tear it down.

In the same way, when you assign a copyright, you transfer your title to the new owner (like a publisher or a film studio). That party now controls that right for the entire remainder of the copyright term, which in most countries is the life of the author plus 70 years. The original owner, the author, is gone from the ownership equation.

A valid assignment has a high legal bar. Because it is a complete transfer of ownership, the law requires it to be in writing and signed by the copyright owner (or their authorized agent). A verbal agreement to "sell" your copyright is almost always unenforceable. This is a critical protection for authors.

Why would an author ever assign their work? In some cases, a large, one-time, lump-sum payment is more appealing than a long-term, uncertain stream of royalties. An author might sell the film rights to their novel (a derivative work) to a studio in an all-encompassing assignment. The studio pays a large fee, but they now own those film rights completely. They can make a movie, a sequel, or a TV show based on it without further payment to the author, other than what was in that initial contract.

Another common form of assignment is a "work made for hire" agreement. When an employee creates something as part of their job, or when a freelancer signs a specific "work for hire" contract, the law states that the employer or commissioning party is considered the author and owner from the moment of creation. This is, in effect, a complete and automatic assignment of all rights.

A License: The Rental of Your Property

A license, on the other hand, is not a sale. It is a grant of permission to use a copyrighted work in certain, specified ways for a limited period, all while the author retains ownership.

This is like renting out your property. If you rent your house to a tenant, you still own the house. The tenant has a contract (a lease) that allows them to use the property under specific conditions. They can live in the house, but they can't sell it. They can use it for a defined term (e.g., one year). And they must pay you rent (royalties). At the end of the lease, the right to use the house fully reverts to you.

This is the power of a license. The author remains the owner of the copyright. They are simply allowing a publisher to exercise certain rights from the bundle, and only under specific conditions.

For example, an author might grant a publisher:

The exclusive right (the license)

to reproduce and distribute (the rights)

the hardcover and paperback editions (the formats)

of the novel (the work)

in North America (the territory)

for 10 years (the duration)

in exchange for a 10% royalty (the payment).

In this scenario, the author keeps ownership. They can still license the audiobook rights to a different company. They can license the German translation rights to a German publisher. They can license the film rights to a studio. They have successfully "rented out" different rooms of their house to different tenants, maximizing the property's value.

The Modern Trend: Why Licensing is Smarter

While some traditional, old-fashioned publishing agreements might still be structured as broad assignments, the modern trend is overwhelmingly in favor of licenses. This shift has been championed by literary agents and author advocacy groups who understand the long-term value of an author's rights.

Licensing allows the author to retain ultimate ownership and control. It allows them to grant only the specific rights necessary for that specific publisher to bring the book to market. This prevents a publisher from "squatting" on rights they have no intention of using. For instance, why grant a small print publisher your film rights? They have no expertise in selling them. It is far better to reserve those rights and sell them yourself (or through a specialized film agent) when the time is right.

Furthermore, a license is almost always tied to performance. If the publisher fails to publish the book within a certain time, or if the book goes out of print, a well-drafted license agreement allows the author to terminate the contract and get their rights back. This is called a "reversion of rights." With an assignment, this is nearly impossible. Once you sell your property, you cannot just ask for it back if the new owner lets the lawn get overgrown.

In short, an assignment is a single transaction. A license is the foundation of a long-term business partnership. For an author who believes in the long-term value of their work, a license is almost always the superior strategic choice.

Sub-topic 12.2: Key Terms in a Publishing Agreement: Grant of Rights Clause

The "Grant of Rights" clause is the heart of any publishing agreement. It is often the most densely worded and heavily negotiated section of the entire contract, and for good reason. This clause is the engine of the deal. It is the section that defines precisely which rights from the author's "bundle of rights" are being transferred to the publisher, under what conditions, and for how long.

Authors and their representatives must scrutinize this clause with extreme care, word by word. A single ambiguous phrase can cost an author millions of dollars or control of their creative legacy. This clause is where the abstract concepts of "assignment vs. license" become concrete reality.

Here is a detailed breakdown of the key elements you must analyze and negotiate.

Scope of Rights: What Are You Actually Granting?

This element specifies exactly which rights are being granted. A publisher will naturally ask for as many rights as possible. The author's job is to grant as few rights as necessary for that publisher to do their specific job.

Primary Rights: These are the main rights the publisher is acquiring, usually "print publication" rights. The contract should list them.

Ancillary/Subsidiary Rights: This is where the real danger lies. Publishers will often try to acquire a long list of other rights, such as audiobook, ebook, first serial (publishing an excerpt before the book's release), second serial, large print, book club, merchandising, and even film/TV rights.

The author must ask: Does this publisher have a concrete plan, a strong track record, and the in-house capacity to actually exploit these rights? Or will they simply sub-license them to another company and take a large cut (often 50%) of the income for doing very little work? In many cases, it is far more profitable for the author to reserve these rights and sell them separately.

A major red flag is any broad, "all-encompassing" language. Be extremely wary of clauses that grant the publisher "all rights in the work," "all media rights," or the most dangerous of all: rights in all formats "now known or hereafter devised." This "hereafter devised" language is how publishers claimed ebook rights in the 1990s from contracts signed in the 1970s, long before anyone imagined a Kindle. Authors should always strike this language. If a new technology comes along, the publisher should have to come back to the author and negotiate a new deal for it.

Exclusivity: Are They the Only One?

A license can be exclusive or non-exclusive.

Exclusive: This means only that publisher can exercise the granted right. For primary print rights, this is standard and reasonable. A publisher needs to know they are the only ones printing the hardcover in the U.S.

Non-Exclusive: This means the author can grant the same right to other parties. This is rare for primary rights but can be useful for certain subsidiary rights, like the right to use excerpts for promotion.

The danger of an exclusive grant is that if the publisher fails to exploit it, that right is locked up. For example, if you grant "exclusive audiobook rights" and the publisher never produces an audiobook, you cannot go to another company to get it done. This is why exclusivity must be tied to a strong reversion clause.

Territory: Where in the World?

This defines the geographic scope of the grant. A publisher might ask for "World rights." This is often a bad deal for the author. A U.S.-based publisher, for example, may have excellent distribution in North America but very weak connections in the United Kingdom, Australia, or India.

It is almost always better to break up the territory. An author can grant:

"United States and Canada" rights to a U.S. publisher.

"United Kingdom and Commonwealth" (excluding Canada) rights to a U.K. publisher.

Separately retain and sell translation rights, territory by territory (e.g., German-language rights to a German publisher, Spanish-language rights to a Spanish publisher, etc.).

This approach allows the author to partner with local experts in each market, resulting in better marketing, better sales, and a higher overall income.

Duration: How Long Do They Have It?

This specifies the term of the license. The publisher's default request will often be "for the full term of copyright" (life of the author plus 70 years). This is an incredibly long time. An author should never agree to this unless it is tied to a powerful reversion clause.

A much better, though rarer, deal is a fixed-term license, such as "seven (7) years from the date of first publication." This creates a specific date when the author gets their rights back, allowing them to re-sell the book to the highest bidder if it's still successful, or take it to a new publisher if the first one did a poor job.

The Reversion Clause: Your Most Important Protection

Since most publishers insist on a "full term of copyright" grant, the reversion clause (also called a termination clause) is your most critical safeguard. This clause states that the rights will "revert" to the author if the publisher fails to meet certain obligations.

The most common trigger is the book going "out of print." But the definition of "out of print" is a trap. In the digital age, a publisher can claim a book is never out of print because it is technically "available" via a print-on-demand (POD) service or as an ebook, even if it sells zero copies.

A good, modern reversion clause must be based on performance. It should state that the book is deemed "out of print" if the publisher sells fewer than a specific number of copies (e.g., 250 copies) in a 12-month royalty period. This gives the author a clear, objective benchmark to meet. If sales fall below that level, the author can send a written notice to the publisher, who then has a short window (e.g., 3-6 months) to either re-launch the book or release the rights. This clause is the author's escape hatch from a failing partnership, and it is absolutely essential.

Part 1 (Sub-topic 12.3): Negotiating for the Future: Reversion Clauses and the Right of Termination

Signing a publishing contract is an act of faith. An author hands over their creation, their "book baby," to a publisher, trusting them to be a good partner for years, or even decades.

But what happens when that partnership fades?

What happens when your publisher, who was so enthusiastic in year one, has moved on to a new, best-selling author in year ten? Your book, which is still your legacy and a potential source of income, is now just a file on a server. It's not being marketed. It's not in bookstores. It's effectively sitting in a digital basement, locked away by a contract you signed a long time ago.

This is where planning for the future becomes the most important thing you can do. You need an escape hatch. In publishing, you have two: one you negotiate (the reversion clause) and one that is given to you by law (the right of termination).

The Reversion Clause: Your Contractual Escape Hatch

This clause is your first and most important line of defense. Traditionally, it was called an "out-of-print" clause.

In the old days, this was simple. A book was "in print" if the publisher had physical copies in a warehouse. If they ran out of copies and decided not to print more, the book was officially "out of print." At that point, the author could send a letter, and the rights would revert back to them.

Then, technology broke this completely.

Two things made the old "out-of-print" clause totally useless: ebooks and print-on-demand (POD).

Today, a book can never be "out of print." As long as the publisher has a digital file (for an ebook) or has it listed with a POD service (where a single copy is printed every time someone orders it), they can legally claim the book is still "in print."

This creates a nightmare scenario. There are authors today whose books are selling 10 or 20 copies a year, earning them almost nothing. Yet, because the book is technically "available for sale" as an ebook, the publisher refuses to return the rights. The publisher has no incentive to market it, but they also have no incentive to give it back. They are, in effect, squatting on the author's copyright.

The Modern Solution: Sales-Based Reversion

Because of this, a modern, well-negotiated contract must not define "out of print" by "availability." It must define it by performance.

You need to negotiate a clause that is tied to actual sales figures or income.

A good, author-friendly clause will look something like this:

"The Work will be considered 'out-of-print' if, after the first two (2) years of publication, the total number of copies sold in all formats (print and electronic) falls below 250 copies in a 12-month period."

Or, it could be based on money earned:

"...if the total income paid to the Author from sales of the Work is less than $200 in any two (2) consecutive six-month royalty periods."

These numbers (250 copies or $200) are just examples; they can be higher or lower depending on the publisher. But the principle is what matters. It creates a clear, objective trigger. If the publisher is not actively and successfully selling the book above this minimum level, the author has the right to ask for their rights back.

How to Use Your Reversion Clause

Even when you have this clause, it's almost never automatic. You, the author, have to be the one to activate it.

Monitor Your Statements: You must read your royalty statements. When you see that the sales have dropped below the threshold, you can act.

Send a Formal Notice: You can't just call your old editor. You must send a formal, written notice to the publisher (usually to their legal or contracts department). You should send this by email and by certified mail with a return receipt. This creates a paper trail.

Be Polite and Professional: The letter should be simple. "Dear [Publisher], per section [Clause Number] of my agreement dated [Date], sales of my book [Title] have fallen below the [Number] copy threshold in the last 12-month period. I am hereby providing written notice to request that all rights granted under this agreement revert to me."

The "Right to Cure": Be aware that many publishers will add a "right to cure" to this clause. This means that after you send your notice, they have a set period (like 6-12 months) to "cure" the problem. They might run a 99-cent ebook sale or a small ad campaign to get the sales numbers back over the threshold. This is a common tactic to watch out for.

The Right of Termination: Your Legal "Second Bite"

Now, let's talk about the big one. This isn't part of your contract. This is a part of U.S. Copyright Law.

Congress recognized that authors and creators often have very little bargaining power at the beginning of their careers. They sign deals they later regret, handing over their rights for their entire lifetime plus 70 years.

To fix this, the Copyright Act of 1976 created a "statutory safety net" called the Right of Termination.

This law gives authors (or their families) a one-time chance to terminate an old grant of rights and take their copyright back. It's often called the "second bite at the apple."

Here's how it works:

For any publishing agreement signed on or after January 1, 1978, the author has a five-year window to terminate that agreement, and that window opens 35 years after the grant was made.

Let's make that simple:

You sign a book deal in 1990.

Your 35-year clock starts.

In 2025 (35 years later), your five-year window opens.

This means that between 2025 and 2030, you (or your heirs) can legally terminate the 1990 contract and reclaim your copyright.

This is an incredibly powerful tool. A book you sold for a small advance in 1990 might now be a perfect fit for a Netflix series. By terminating the old grant, you can reclaim the rights and re-sell them at 2025 prices.

The "Inalienable" Superpower

Here is the most important part of the termination right: it is inalienable.

This means you cannot waive it. You cannot trade it away.

Even if your 1990 contract includes a sentence that says, "The author hereby agrees to waive their statutory right of termination," that sentence is legally void and unenforceable. The law passed by Congress is stronger than a private contract.

This right belongs to you, no matter what you signed.

The Process and the "Work for Hire" Exception

There are two major catches.

First, this is not a simple process. You cannot just send a letter. It is a formal, legal proceeding. You must serve a written notice of termination on the publisher in a very specific time frame (no less than 2 years and no more than 10 years before your chosen termination date). You must also file that notice with the U.S. Copyright Office. You absolutely must hire an experienced copyright lawyer to handle this.

Second, it does not apply to "works made for hire." If you were an employee of a company writing a manual, you can't terminate. Or, if your contract specifically (and legally) defined your book as a "work for hire" (this is rare for novels but can happen with non-fiction or contributions), you are not considered the "author" under the law, and you don't have this right.

In summary, the reversion clause is your short-term tool to save a book that is underperforming now. The right of termination is your long-term, powerful, legal tool to reclaim your life's work for yourself and your family.

Part 2 (Sub-topic 12.4): The Creative Commons Licensing Framework

For decades, the world of copyright was black and white. You had two choices:

All Rights Reserved: This is traditional copyright. It's a giant legal wall. It means, "This work is mine. If you want to use it in any way—share it, copy it, translate it, put it in your blog—you must find me and ask my permission (and probably pay me)."

Public Domain: This is the opposite. It's a wide-open field. The work belongs to everyone. You can do anything you want with it, and you don't have to ask permission or credit anyone.

This system works well for commercial entertainment, like blockbuster movies or best-selling novels. But what about other creators?

What about a scientist who wants her research to be shared as widely as possible? What about a teacher who creates a textbook and wants other teachers to adapt it for their own classes? What about a photographer who just wants people to use her photos, as long as they say where they got them?

For these people, "All Rights Reserved" is a problem. It's a barrier to the very dissemination they want.

This is why Creative Commons (CC) was born.

Creative Commons is not an alternative to copyright. It is a system that works with copyright. It allows a creator to change their message from "All Rights Reserved" to "Some Rights Reserved."

When an author applies a CC license to their work, they are not giving up their copyright. They are still the owner. They are simply giving the public permission, in advance, to use their work under a clear set of rules. It's like putting a welcome mat on your door with a sign that says, "Come on in! Just make sure to credit me and don't try to sell my furniture."

The Four Building Blocks of CC Licenses

The entire Creative Commons system is built by mixing and matching four simple conditions.

1. BY (Attribution)

Icon:

What it means: This is the foundation of all CC licenses. It simply says, "You can use my work, but you must give me credit (attribution) in the way I request." This is the most basic rule of academic and creative courtesy. A good attribution includes the work's Title, its Author, its Source (like a web link), and its License (e.g., "CC BY").

2. SA (ShareAlike)

Icon:

What it means: This is the "pay it forward" condition. It says, "You can adapt or 'remix' my work to create a new work. But if you do, your new creation must be shared under the exact same 'ShareAlike' license." This is what helps the "commons" of free content grow. The most famous example is Wikipedia. Its content is CC BY-SA, which means you can use its text, but your project must also be CC BY-SA.

3. NC (NonCommercial)

Icon:

What it means: This is the "for love, not money" rule. It says, "You can use my work, but you cannot use it for commercial purposes." A student can use your CC BY-NC photo in a school report (non-commercial). But a company cannot use that same photo in a magazine advertisement (commercial).

4. ND (NoDerivatives)

Icon:

What it means: This is the "look, don't touch" (or "share, but don't change") rule. It says, "You can copy and share my work, but you cannot modify, adapt, or 'remix' it in any way." You can't translate the work, or use a sample of the song in your own mix, or crop the photo. It must be passed along, whole and unchanged.

The Six Main Creative Commons Licenses

By combining these four building blocks, we get the six main CC licenses. They are often listed in order from most open to most restrictive.

1. CC BY (Attribution)

This is the most open and accommodating license. It lets people do anything they want with your work—distribute it, change it, and even use it commercially—as long as they give you credit. This is the gold standard for open-access academic publishing and government data.

2. CC BY-SA (Attribution-ShareAlike)

This is the "Wikipedia" license. It lets people do anything they want with your work (even commercially), as long as they credit you and license their new creation under the same CC BY-SA terms.

3. CC BY-NC (Attribution-NonCommercial)

This is very popular with artists and photographers. It lets people use, share, and remix your work, but only for non-commercial purposes. They must still credit you.

4. CC BY-ND (Attribution-NoDerivatives)

This license allows for sharing, even commercially, but the work cannot be changed at all. People can copy and share your essay, but they can't translate it or abridge it. They must credit you and share the original, unmodified work.

5. CC BY-NC-SA (Attribution-NonCommercial-ShareAlike)

This is getting more restrictive. It lets people remix and build upon your work, but only for non-commercial purposes, and they must credit you, and they must license their new creation under these same identical terms.

6. CC BY-NC-ND (Attribution-NonCommercial-NoDerivatives)

This is the most restrictive of the six licenses. It is the closest to "All Rights Reserved." It basically says, "You can download my work and share it with others for free, as long as you credit me. But you cannot change it in any way, and you cannot use it for commercial purposes."

One Special Case: CC0 (Public Domain Dedication)

There is one other tool that is even more open than CC BY. It's called CC0 (CC Zero).

CC0 is not a license; it's a waiver. It's the creator's way of saying, "I give up all my copyright in this work. I dedicate it to the public domain. Do whatever you want with it, for any reason, and you don't even have to credit me."

This is an act of "no rights reserved." It's used by museums like the New York's Metropolitan Museum of Art, which uses CC0 to release high-resolution images of paintings that are already in the public domain, making them unambiguously free for anyone to use.

Ultimately, the Creative Commons framework is a set of flexible tools. It gives authors the power to choose exactly how they want their work to be used, moving beyond a simple "on/off" switch and into a spectrum of sharing and control.

Part V: Enforcement and the Future

Defending Your Work: Understanding Infringement and Enforcement

Defending Your Work: Understanding Infringement and Enforcement

Owning a copyright is of little value without the ability to defend it against unauthorized use. Copyright infringement occurs when a third party violates one of the exclusive rights granted to the copyright owner—such as the right to reproduce, distribute, or adapt the work—without permission. This chapter provides a practical overview of what constitutes infringement and the escalating series of remedies available to a rights holder, from informal notices to formal litigation.

Sub-topic 13.1: What Constitutes Infringement: Direct, Contributory, and Vicarious

Copyright law is designed to be comprehensive. It understands that infringement isn't always a simple, one-person act. Sometimes, one person commits the act, another person encourages them, and a third person profits from it all. To address this reality, the law recognizes several types of infringement, which allows a copyright holder to target not only the primary copier but also the systems and businesses that enable and profit from the theft.

Let's break down the three main categories.

Direct Infringement

This is the most common and straightforward type of infringement. It's what most people think of when they hear the term. Direct infringement is committed by the person who, or entity that, actually performs the unauthorized act.

An individual scans your entire novel and uploads the PDF to a file-sharing website.

A company takes a photograph you posted on your blog and uses it in a commercial advertisement without your permission.

A musician covers your song and sells it on their album without first obtaining a mechanical license.

A local theater performs your play without paying licensing fees.

The most important concept here is that liability for direct infringement is "strict." This is a crucial legal term. It means the infringer's intent or knowledge does not matter. The person who used your photo in their ad can't successfully argue, "But I didn't know it was copyrighted!" or "I thought it was free to use!" The simple fact is that they did use it, and that act violated your exclusive right. Their lack of knowledge might affect how much they have to pay in damages (which we'll cover later), but it doesn't absolve them of liability. The act itself is the violation.

Contributory Infringement

This is the first layer of "secondary" liability. It targets the enablers. A party is liable for contributory infringement if they meet two specific conditions:

They have knowledge of the direct infringing activity.

They intentionally induce or materially contribute to that activity.

The classic example from the early days of the internet was Napster. The company running the file-sharing service knew its users were engaging in direct infringement (sharing copyrighted music). The company materially contributed by providing the entire platform—the software, the servers, and the search tools—that made the infringement possible.

In the book example, the person who uploaded the PDF is the direct infringer. The operator of the website who knows the PDF is pirated, keeps it on their server, and provides a "Download" button is the contributory infringer. They are contributing to the violation. This is different from a neutral service provider, like a basic internet service provider or a cloud storage company, that simply provides automated services without specific knowledge of what a user is doing. Contributory infringement requires that element of knowledge and active assistance.

Vicarious Infringement

This is the second type of "secondary" liability, and it targets those who profit from infringement, even if they don't actively help it. Liability for vicarious infringement attaches to a party who has two different things:

The right and ability to supervise the direct infringer's activity.

A direct financial benefit from the infringement.

Notice that knowledge is not a required element here. This is about profiting from an activity you could have stopped.

The prompt's example of a flea market owner is perfect. The owner rents out stalls to vendors. One vendor is selling counterfeit, pirated copies of your book. The owner has the right and ability to supervise—they are the landlord, they can walk the aisles, and they have a rental agreement that certainly allows them to kick out a vendor for illegal activity. The owner also gets a direct financial benefit—they get rent from that specific vendor. Even if the owner claims, "I never knew what they were selling," they could still be held vicariously liable because they profited from an infringement they had the power to stop.

This also applies to a dance hall owner who hires a live band. The band (the direct infringer) plays copyrighted songs without a license. The hall owner has the right to supervise (they hired the band and can control the event) and gets a direct financial benefit (ticket sales). The owner is vicariously liable for the band's infringement.

These secondary liability rules are essential. They give copyright owners the power to go after the larger, more established businesses that facilitate and monetize piracy, rather than just playing an endless game of whack-a-mole with individual users.

Sub-topic 13.2: The Enforcement Toolkit: Cease-and-Desist Letters and Takedown Notices

When you discover someone is infringing on your copyright, your first instinct might be to file a lawsuit. However, in most cases, that is not the first, best, or most cost-effective step. Before resorting to the time and expense of federal court, a copyright owner has a powerful toolkit of pre-litigation measures that resolve the vast majority of disputes.

The Cease-and-Desist (C&D) Letter

The first step is almost always a formal letter. A cease-and-desist letter, often called a "demand letter," is a formal written communication sent directly to the alleged infringer. It is not a court order, but it is a serious legal document that functions as a "shot across the bow."

A well-drafted C&D letter accomplishes several things at once:

It Identifies the Work: It clearly states what copyrighted work is being infringed (e.g., "my novel, The Last Horizon, U.S. Copyright Registration No. TX 1-234-567").

It Details the Infringement: It explains exactly what the infringer is doing wrong (e.g., "You are distributing an unauthorized PDF copy of my novel on your website at the URL...").

It Makes a Demand: It clearly demands that the infringer "cease" (stop) the infringing activity and "desist" (not do it in the future). It may also demand compensation for the harm already caused or an accounting of all profits made.

It Sets a Deadline: It gives the infringer a specific, reasonable timeframe (e.g., 10 business days) to comply.

It Creates a Record: This is critical. If the infringer ignores the letter and continues their activity, it becomes much easier to prove "willful infringement" in court later, which can lead to much higher damages. The infringer can no longer claim they "didn't know."

While you can write a C&D letter yourself, a letter sent from an attorney's office on official letterhead carries significantly more weight. It signals to the infringer that you are serious, you know your rights, and you are prepared to escalate the matter. Many infringers, especially those who are casual or ignorant of the law, will comply immediately to avoid a lawsuit.

The DMCA Takedown Notice

In the online world, the most powerful tool is the takedown notice, established by the Digital Millennium Copyright Act (DMCA). The DMCA created a brilliant legal trade-off called a "safe harbor." In short, it protects online service providers (OSPs)—like YouTube, Facebook, Google, and web hosting companies—from being held liable for the infringing content their users post.

However, to qualify for this "safe harbor" protection, the OSP must follow a strict set of rules. The most important rule is that they must "expeditiously remove or disable access to" infringing material as soon as they receive a valid takedown notice from the copyright owner.

This "notice-and-takedown" system is the engine of modern online copyright enforcement. The process works like this:

You find your copyrighted book, photo, or song on a platform.

You send a formal DMCA Takedown Notice to that platform's designated DMCA Agent (this contact info is usually in their "Legal" or "Terms of Service" page).

Your notice must contain specific legal elements, including your contact information, a description of your work, the exact location (URL) of the infringing material, and a statement under penalty of perjury that you are the copyright owner (or authorized to act for them).

Once the OSP receives this valid notice, they are legally obligated to remove the content quickly.

This allows a creator to get their work removed from a major platform in a matter of hours or days, without needing a lawyer or a court order.

It's also important to know about the "counter-notice." The user who posted the content can send a counter-notice to the OSP, claiming under penalty of perjury that the content was removed by mistake or is protected by fair use. If this happens, the OSP notifies you, the copyright owner. You then have approximately 10 to 14 business days to file a formal lawsuit against that user. If you don't file a lawsuit in that window, the OSP is allowed to put the content back up. This system protects both copyright holders from infringement and users from fraudulent or mistaken takedown notices.

Sub-topic 13.3: Legal Remedies: Injunctions, Damages, and Criminal Penalties

If cease-and-desist letters are ignored and takedown notices are ineffective (perhaps because the infringer is hosting their own website), the copyright owner's final recourse is to file a lawsuit in federal court. If the court finds that infringement has indeed occurred, it has a wide range of powerful remedies it can award. These remedies are designed to stop the infringement, compensate the owner for their losses, and, in some cases, punish the infringer.

Injunctions

An injunction is a formal, binding court order that compels a party to do or, more commonly, to stop doing something. This is often the most important and immediate goal of a lawsuit: to make the infringement stop, right now.

Temporary Restraining Order (TRO): This is an emergency order. A court can issue it at the very beginning of a case, sometimes even without the infringer being present, to stop immediate and irreversible harm (e.g., to stop the distribution of a pirated movie on its opening weekend).

Preliminary Injunction: This is a more stable order issued after both sides have had a chance to argue. It typically remains in effect for the entire duration of the lawsuit, which can take months or years.

Permanent Injunction: This is the final order issued at the end of the case if the copyright owner wins. It permanently forbids the infringer from ever engaging in the infringing activity again.

Violating a court injunction is a very serious matter. It's not just a civil dispute anymore; it's contempt of court, which can lead to severe fines and even jail time.

Monetary Damages

The court will also award monetary damages to compensate the copyright owner. The owner generally gets to choose between two different types of damages, whichever is more beneficial for them.

Actual Damages and Profits: This award is designed to make the copyright owner "whole." It consists of two parts:

Actual Damages: The amount of money the copyright owner lost because of the infringement. This could be lost sales, damage to their brand, or a drop in their own licensing fees.

Infringer's Profits: Any profits the infringer made from the unauthorized use (that aren't already counted in the actual damages).
The problem? This can be very difficult to prove. How do you prove exactly how many sales you would have made? It often requires expensive financial experts and complex calculations.

Statutory Damages: Because actual damages are so hard to prove, U.S. copyright law provides an incredibly powerful alternative: statutory damages. To be eligible for this, the copyright owner must have registered their work with the U.S. Copyright Office before the infringement began (or within three months of the work's publication).

If you are eligible, you can ask the court for statutory damages instead of proving your losses. The court can then award a pre-set amount for each work infringed.

The standard range is $750 to $30,000 per work.

If the infringer proves they were "innocent" (had no idea they were infringing), the court can lower this to $200.

If the copyright owner proves the infringement was "willful" (e.g., the infringer ignored a C&D letter), the court can raise the amount to $150,000 per work.

Think about that. If someone willfully infringes on a collection of 10 of your registered photographs, they could be on the hook for up to $1.5 million, plus...

Attorney's Fees and Costs: In addition to damages, a (timely) registered copyright also makes you eligible to have the court order the infringer to pay for all of your court costs and reasonable attorney's fees. This is a massive hammer, as legal fees can often exceed the damages themselves. The availability of statutory damages and attorney's fees is the single biggest reason for all creators to register their work.

Criminal Penalties

Most copyright disputes are civil matters between two parties. But in the most extreme cases, the government itself can bring criminal charges. This is reserved for willful infringement on a commercial scale, such as running a massive pirate website or manufacturing and selling thousands of counterfeit books. The penalties are severe, including hundreds of thousands of dollars in fines and several years in federal prison.

Sub-topic 13.4: International Enforcement and Anti-Piracy Measures

In our connected, digital world, piracy is a global problem. The internet has no borders, but copyright laws do. This creates the biggest challenge in modern enforcement:

what do you do when the person infringing your work is operating a website from a server in a country that has weak intellectual property laws or simply refuses to cooperate with a U.S. court order? A U.S. judge's injunction is worthless against an anonymous operator in a non-cooperative jurisdiction.

To combat this, rights holders, industries, and governments have developed a multi-pronged approach to attack the problem from different angles.

Legislative Site-Blocking

As the prompt mentions, one increasingly common strategy is "site-blocking." This approach, used effectively in many countries like the United Kingdom, Australia, and across the European Union, targets the access to a pirate site rather than the site itself.

Here's how it works: A copyright holder (like a publisher or movie studio) goes to a federal court in their own country. They provide evidence that a foreign website (e.g., "pirate-books-for-free.xyz") is "dedicated to piracy." If the judge agrees, the court doesn't try to order the foreign site to shut down. Instead, it issues an order to all the domestic Internet Service Providers (ISPs)—like Comcast, Verizon, and AT&T in the U.S.—commanding them to block their customers from being able to access that specific website.

This doesn't take the pirate site offline, but it effectively makes it invisible and inaccessible to the vast majority of the public within that country, crippling its audience and business model. This is the kind of mechanism proposed in legislative efforts like the one mentioned in the prompt.

Border Control for Physical Goods

For authors and publishers, digital piracy is only half the battle. Counterfeit physical books, printed cheaply overseas and sold online, are a massive problem. This is where U.S. Customs and Border Protection (CBP) becomes a critical partner.

If you have a U.S. copyright registration, you can "record" that registration with CBP for a fee. You provide them with information about your book, what the genuine copies look like, and what known counterfeits look like. With this information in their database, CBP agents at all U.S. ports of entry—at airports, seaports, and international mail facilities—are empowered to identify, seize, and destroy shipments of infringing physical goods. This stops the counterfeit products at the border, before they can ever be sold to a single U.S. customer.

Industry-Led Initiatives

Finally, industry groups often pursue strategies that don't rely on courts at all. A popular and effective method is the "follow the money" approach. Pirate sites need money to operate; they get it from ad revenue and, sometimes, from subscription fees or donations. Anti-piracy groups work directly with major payment processors (like Visa, MasterCard, and PayPal) and advertising networks (like Google's AdSense) to identify pirate sites and cut off their revenue. By convincing these financial partners to terminate their services, the pirate site can be starved of the funds it needs to pay for its servers, effectively shutting it down without a single lawsuit.

Permissible Use: Navigating Fair Use, Fair Dealing, and Other Exceptions

14.1 The U.S. Doctrine of Fair Use: The Four Factors

In the world of copyright, the United States takes a unique path. Instead of creating a strict list of "you can do this" exceptions, U.S. law uses a flexible concept called fair use. This doctrine is found in Section 107 of the Copyright Act.

It's important to understand that fair use isn't a "right" you have. You can't just claim it and be safe. Instead, it's an affirmative defense. This means if a copyright owner sues you for infringement, you can raise your hand in court and say, "Yes, I used the work, but my use was fair." A judge then has to decide if you're right.

To make this decision, the court looks at the specific facts of your case and balances four key factors. No single factor is a magic bullet; they are all weighed together.

1. The Purpose and Character of the Use

This factor asks why you used the work. Courts generally favor uses that are for public-benefit purposes, like non-profit, educational, scholarly, or research uses. If your use is commercial—meaning you're trying to make money from it—you'll have a harder time proving it's fair.

The most crucial part of this factor today is whether your use is "transformative." This is a very important idea. A transformative use is one that doesn't just copy the original. It adds something new. It changes the original work by giving it a new meaning, a new message, or a new expression.

Think about it this way. If you scan a chapter of a Harry Potter book and post it online for people to read, that's not transformative. You've just substituted for the original. But if you're a literary critic and you quote a few paragraphs from that same chapter in a book review to analyze the author's style, that is transformative. You've used the original to create something new: a critical analysis. Parody, which we'll discuss later, is another classic example of a transformative use.

2. The Nature of the Copyrighted Work

This factor looks at the original work you used. The law gives more protection to works that are highly creative. It's more likely to be fair use to quote from a non-fiction historical textbook or a factual news article than it is to copy a large section of a highly imaginative novel, a poem, or a blockbuster movie. The law wants to protect the "creative spark" at the heart of artistic works.

Another key part of this factor is whether the original work was published or unpublished. Courts are very protective of an author's right to be the first person to show their work to the world. Using parts of someone's private, unpublished diary is much, much less likely to be considered fair use than quoting from their published autobiography.

3. The Amount and Substantiality of the Portion Used

This factor is a bit misleading. It's not just about percentages. It looks at both how much you took (quantity) and what part you took (quality).

Using a small, insignificant piece of a work is better than using a large portion. If you use a 10-second, random clip from a 2-hour movie, that's a small amount. But this factor also considers "substantiality." This means you can get into trouble even if you take a tiny piece, if that piece is the "heart of the work."

For example, imagine a mystery movie where the entire plot builds up to a 5-second shot revealing the killer. If your "review" just shows that 5-second clip, you've taken a quantitatively tiny amount, but you've taken the most substantial, most important part of the entire film. That would likely weigh heavily against fair use.

4. The Effect of the Use upon the Potential Market

This factor is often called the most important one. It asks a simple question: Does your new work harm the market for the original? Does it act as a substitute?

If your use would stop people from buying the original work, that's a major problem. This is why posting that Harry Potter chapter online is a problem; it directly substitutes for buying the book. However, a critical review that quotes the book doesn't substitute for it. In fact, a good (or even a bad) review might encourage more people to buy the book to see for themselves.

The same goes for a parody. No one is going to watch the movie Spaceballs instead of watching Star Wars. They are different products for different markets. The parody doesn't steal the original's audience.

Because all four of these factors are flexible and must be balanced, fair use is famously ambiguous and hard to predict. What one judge thinks is fair, another might not. This flexibility is its greatest strength (it can adapt to new technology) and its greatest weakness (it provides very little certainty).

14.2 Fair Dealing in the Commonwealth: A More Prescriptive Approach

While the U.S. has its open-ended "fair use," many other countries, particularly those in the Commonwealth (like the United Kingdom, Canada, and Australia), use a different system called fair dealing.

On the surface, it sounds similar, but it works in a fundamentally different way. Fair dealing is much more structured, more rigid, and less flexible than its American counterpart. It's what lawyers call a "prescriptive" approach. It doesn't start with a vague idea of "fairness"; it starts with a very specific, closed list of rules.

To claim fair dealing, you must pass a two-step test.

Step One: Is Your Purpose on the List?

This is the first and most important hurdle. The law in each country provides a specific, exhaustive list of permitted purposes. If your reason for using the work is not on that list, your use is copyright infringement. The analysis stops right there. It doesn't matter how "fair" or "transformative" your use might seem. If the purpose isn't on the list, you fail.

What's on the list? It varies slightly by country, but the most common permitted purposes are:

- Research
- Private study
- Criticism
- Review

News reporting

Some countries have added others. For instance, Canada's list is a bit broader and includes "parody," "satire," and "education." In the UK, parody, caricature, and pastiche are also now included as specific exceptions.

But this "list" system is the key difference. In the U.S., a court can find any use to be "fair," even if it's for a purpose no one has ever thought of before. Under fair dealing, if your purpose is, for example, "to make a cool art collage" and "art collage" isn't on the country's list, you're out of luck.

Step Two: Was the Dealing "Fair"?

If—and only if—you pass step one, the court then moves on to step two. It determines if your use was actually "fair." This part of the test looks very similar to the U.S. fair use factors.

A court will consider things like:

The amount taken: Did you use more than you needed to for your permitted purpose (like criticism or review)?

The effect on the market: Does your use compete with the original work and harm its sales?

The nature of the work: Was it a creative work? Was it unpublished?

The character of the dealing: How was the work used? Was it for a commercial purpose?

So, while the "fairness" analysis is similar, the entire system is much more restrictive because of that mandatory first.

About Author

Azhar ul Haque Sario is a bestselling author and data scientist with a remarkable record of achievement. This Cambridge alumnus brings a wealth of knowledge to his work, holding an MBA (SZABIST), ACCA (Knowledge Level - FTMS College Malaysia and London College of Accountancy, London), BBA, and several Google certifications, including specializations in Google Data Analytics, Google Digital Marketing & E-commerce, and Google Project Management.

With ten years of business experience, Azhar combines practical expertise with his impressive academic background to craft insightful books. His prolific writing has resulted in an astounding 2810 published titles, earning him the record for the maximum Kindle editions and paperback books published by an individual author in one year, awarded by Asia Books of Records in 2024.

ORCID: https://orcid.org/0009-0004-8629-830X
Azhar.sario@hotmail.co.uk
https://www.linkedin.com/in/azharulhaquesario/

www.ingramcontent.com/pod-product-compliance
Lightning Source LLC
Chambersburg PA
CBHW031346230926
51848CB00002B/412
* 9 7 8 3 3 8 4 7 4 2 6 6 7 *